Philosophies of Spiritual Leaders

Insight and Guidance To Strengthen Your Relationship With God

By Christy Rutherford

Philosophies of Iconic Leaders

ISBN-13: 978-1540528698
ISBN-10: 1540528693

First Edition for Print November 2016

DEDICATION

God, for never leaving me or forsaking me

My family, for unconditional love and support

Table of Contents

Foreword..i

Preface iii

Chapter 1 TD Jakes.. 1

Chapter 2 Joel Osteen.. 11

Chapter 3 Paulo Coelho 19

Chapter 4 Joyce Meyer 27

Chapter 5 John Gray 33

Chapter 6 Neville Goddard...................................... 41

Chapter 7 Sarah Jakes Roberts............................... 49

Chapter 8 Steven Furtick... 55

Chapter 9 Iyanla Vanzant.. 63

Chapter 10 Keion Henderson 71

Closing.. 77

About The Author 78

Foreword

Spirituality is a touching topic. It is the essence of all that we are, and the only right path to fulfillment. But, spirituality has a different meaning for everyone. For me, it is an introduction to who I am... The true me... The "I" that exists and remains behind all my thoughts and emotions, but that continues to expand and evolve. It is an ever-evolving journey and an ever-enlightening one... With new stages of growth come new perspectives that allow us to see the next horizon. And then at the top of that one, everything expands and changes again, so that we can see the next one... It is the "Holy Grail." We never "arrive."

I now know that I am the sum of all things that never change. I am the consciousness behind all that happens to me, for me, around me and, within me. My purpose for being on earth is purely spiritual expansion... To immerse myself in the environment of those who grow me, and to accept my responsibility to create an environment that contributes to the growth of others. Only this way, we will raise the consciousness of the planet enough to discover the answer to the deeply desired questions, "Who are we?" and "Why are we here?"

Crossing paths with Christy three years ago was nothing short of a divine appointment, that has served us both very well. We come from vastly different backgrounds, belief systems, and ideologies... But, here we are, sharing somewhat of the same path... Both dedicated to our own growth and the value that we could offer this world.

After coming from the military, I was in awe of Christy's ability to break free from the progammings of society, and the demands that had been placed on her during that stage of her life. But I felt a deep sense of peace for her, that she had heard the calling on her life, and more importantly, that she had the courage to answer it!!

I don't believe spiritual journey has anything to do with what we "become." I believe it has EVERYTHING to do with UN-becoming all that we're NOT... Once we UNBECOME everything that society has made us believe we are, we don't need to "become" anything, because we already ARE!!! And so all we then need to do is just be!

I have learned so well that there is a very big difference between "my plan" and "THE Plan." People are sent to us, and experiences are given to us, to teach us the lessons that are necessary for us to follow THE Plan... The one that is much bigger than all of ours.

It's not a matter of "learning," it is a matter of REMEMBERING. Allow those around you to help you find your own light, and then use your light to drown out the darkness in others, so that they too may do the same. Allow the words of all Christy's books to touch you. Don't just "read" them, FEEL them. And let them change you just like I've allowed them to change me.

Thank you for the impact you are having on this world Christy, and for being an example of the path we all need to follow... Our own path!! Much love to you, and to every life you touch.xxx

Holly Nunan
Spiritual Coach, Powerful Parenting Coach
Speaker/Teacher on Consciousness
Author, Australian Mumpreneur

Preface

Over four years ago I entered a very dark time in my life. I had high levels of success, was well known in my organization, had been recognized nationally for my work, and had a six-figure career. I worked hard, led 100's of people and made significant contributions in the lives of others as a mentor.

On the outside, I looked like I had it all, but on the inside, I was as hollow as a chocolate Easter Bunny. If you would have bitten my ears off, there wouldn't have been anything on the inside.

How could a person who "had it all" feel so empty? That's a great question. It's mainly because I lived from the outside in and not inside out. Over my adulthood, life had put a whooping on me. I had more knives in my back than a steak house and people criticized me regularly for my visionary thinking. I didn't know who my real friends were and was paranoid at work, feeling like the men I worked with and those in my organization, thought I didn't deserve my position or the awards I had. Some of them assumed I got to where I was, because I was a black woman, despite working nearly 80 hours a week for at least 10 years.

I fought, bled and nearly worked myself to death to achieve high levels of success and it came at a high cost. I shared the story of how I found myself in darkness in my book, *Shackled To Success*. At a certain point in my journey, I started searching for something, but I couldn't put my finger on what it was.

The biggest challenge I had was unforgiveness. I held on to the past, which created secret resentment, and it only got worse as I moved up in my career and started to get a large number of critics. Anyone who's highly successful is also highly criticized. It's a part of the plan. I was drowning in negativity, while I continued to work hard every day and set new standards. The weight and the pressure from dragging around my past and being harshly criticized from people I thought were my friends had become unbearable.

Can you relate to this picture? Maybe not the hair, but everything else going on in it. I was drowning in the ocean of guilt, resentment and hate (for my haters). The weights that kept me where I was included my family who were so proud of what I accomplished (They bragged to their friends about me. How could I admit I was broken?); friends who had similar issues, so meeting high levels of resistance as minorities was normal, expected and accepted; friends who weren't my real friends because they criticized me; shame from being so unhappy with all that I had; and unforgiveness for anyone who had done me wrong.

Drugs and alcohol were easier to grab than change and forgiveness. Wine was my numbing agent of choice – might as well be healthy. Drugs – not gonna happen. I held the keys my freedom, but drinking wine was easier than forgiving people. Choosing to unlock the weights would allow me to rise above water, which would make change and forgiveness easier, but how do I do that when it's SO HARD??!!

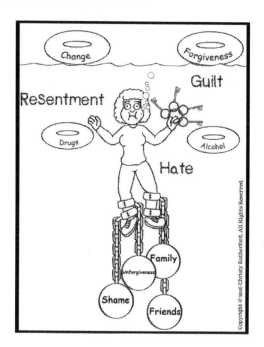

The Surrender

I started praying that God would aid me in my great despair and save me from the secret hell I was living. As a highly regarded leader, I couldn't afford for anyone to know what was going on and that I was unraveling at the seam. I showed up to work every day with a smile on my face and wore a mask to hide the shame of living in a hell that I couldn't seem to get out of. No one checks on the well-being of their heroes and we act as if we are invincible. Since we all have storms at some point, life can eventually catch invincible leaders on the blindside.

One day, I laid in my bed and cried loudly, because my ankle had exploded with arthritis and I couldn't walk. Nearly howling in despair and desperation, I knew that I was being forced to make a decision. One that I dreaded making for a long time. My arthritis was stress induced, and since I didn't manage it properly, it erupted my body in disease and decay. I was at a place in my life that I thought I was going to die.

As I cried and cried, someone said to me, "Put your gloves down Christy. It's time to stop fighting." I answered the voice aloud and said, "Okay, I surrender."

A few days later, I turned in my letter of resignation. Five weeks later, I left my successful career with only three years and six months left to retire with a full pension. I then started on my journey of destiny and BECOMING.

Relationship is Personal

I'm still an amateur on the Bible and will not claim to be a spiritual teacher, but I want to give an account of my personal experience. Really, just an introduction and the rest will be expanded in future books. It's not my intent to offend, discredit, criticize or demean anyone, their religion or beliefs. We are all individual beings and will have personal experiences on who we choose to worship and how we choose to worship them.

For nearly 20 years, I ran away from organized religion. Going to small churches that taught about God from the Old Testament didn't make me feel good. The vibrations were low and I usually felt small and minimized after leaving. Always hearing that God was a jealous God and that I would be punished with hell, fire, and brimstone if I didn't abide by what seemed like impossible standards was scary. Not only that, to see so called "sanctified people" talk about others on an epic level and do negative things, but go to church faithfully every Sunday, turned me off from church all together. I became an atheist.

Over that 20-year period, I didn't acknowledge that God existed but would call upon him when I got into deep trouble. A hypocrite? Yes, I know, but stick with me. I prayed for healing when I was crippled with arthritis in 2001 and was fully healed, without medication. I prayed for several other things and after a series of showing up when I needed Him and then denying Him after I got it, one day I thought, "Maybe there is something to God, but how do I get back?"

Deuteronomy 31:6 (NIV) - "...he will never leave you nor forsake you."

The Journey

For a long time, I thought that highly spiritual people were weird. But, they had peace and I had chaos, so who was the real weirdo? As life continued to wear me out, I felt a positive energy that was pulling me and urging me to get closer. But closer to what? What is it? Who is God? What is He and what can He do for me?

Over six years ago, being introduced to spiritual teachers by Oprah, her guests included Dr. Wayne Dyer, Eckhart Tolle, Lois Hay, Dr. Maya Angelou, Abraham Hicks and Gary Zukav. They talked about an energy, a Being, the source, the universe....God. The Being they talked about wasn't the hell and brimstone person that would cast down the heavens, and burn me up if I ever sinned. They spoke of love, openness, and acceptance.

After hearing about this loving Being, I secretly declared that I wanted to be closer to God and set out on a path to make something happen. I was unsure of how to get closer to something I didn't understand.

The day I lay in my bed and heard the voice, I didn't know who it was. As I've continued to grow and develop spiritually, I've learned that it was the voice of God calling me back to the original path that was set out for me. I had gotten off His Path when I entered my career, but that was not who I was meant to BE. I was meant to be who I am today but had to UNBECOME who I thought I was, in order to BE this person. This story will also be highlighted in future books.

I Wanted God, Not Church

Bishop TD Jakes said, "A third of adults under 30 are religiously unaffiliated. No affiliation, no interest, no concept at all. That's the highest it has ever been since we have been recording data. Our generation has done the worst job of winning our children's generation in the history of the church since data has been collected... Thirteen million self-described atheists and agnostics in America alone...and there are 33 million who say they have no religious affiliation at all... They are 33 million people who say, I may be into God, but I'm not into church."

It's well known that when the student is ready, the teacher will appear. There are a gazillion people ready and willing to teach you the word of God. There are small churches, mega churches, virtual churches, spiritual teachers, podcasts, websites, etc. How you learn should be based on personal preference and personal desires. Also, who you are and what you want to do with your life.

Some people love small churches, and others prefer mega churches. I'm personally not a fan of small churches. I didn't like to stand up and announce my name and where I was from to an established congregation of people that I thought were secretly judging me. I didn't like to see the same people fall out on the floor every Sunday because I was secretly judging them. I didn't like to be in a church where people spoke in tongues because I found it super distracting.

Although I was highly successful in my career, I didn't know any scriptures and felt like a dummy for not knowing the fundamental rituals of church. As a leader, I always had to be conscious of how I was perceived by others. I lost my sense of self during my career and didn't want people talking to me or asking me questions in church, even though they were nice.

I was self-conscious and wanted to experience God, but didn't want people to see me doing it since I didn't do it like them. I wasn't loud and didn't talk. I didn't fall out or speak in tongues. I didn't understand why people raised their hands. I didn't want to raise my hands. I didn't have a Bible because I didn't know how to find the verses.

Finding The Way Back

One day in 2009, I watched Pastor Joel Osteen on television. I was hooked because he didn't quote a bunch of scriptures. He taught how to live a better, more expansive and greater life. I watched his shows periodically and when I moved to Texas a few years later, I drove 1.5 hours to his church a few Sundays a month.

After leaving Texas, I streamed his services live from their website. Over the past three years, I've expanded and watch the other leaders featured in this book. They each have a unique way of teaching and I thoroughly enjoy them.

I can honestly say that watching a multitude of videos from these spiritual teachers has transformed my life and strengthened my connection with God. They are loved by millions all over the world, but interestingly enough, some of them are also highly criticized by others.

Walking in God's Purpose has not spared them from the burden that comes with higher positions of authority and blessings, but I'm glad they persevered through their process and broke the mold in order to Become who they were meant to be in order to serve who they were meant to serve.

You don't have to go to church to get closer or come into relationship with God. You also don't have to walk around quoting scriptures, wear a cross and carry a Bible to get into relationship. It's a personal choice and a personal journey, but learning from other spiritual teachers is the key.

Who Is This Book For?

This book is for anyone who wants insight on how to apply Biblical principles to their everyday life. It's also for anyone who wants to have a relationship with God but is confused on how to do so. This book is in plain language, not scriptural, and shares the lessons that other leaders have learned along their journeys. It's for anyone looking for insight on what other people have struggled with in their lives, and how their healed brokenness is being used by God to serve others.

My goal with this book is to share the principles and philosophies of Spiritual Leaders, to learn from them and use their hindsight to illuminate the road to destiny in front of you.

You'll also get a glimpse into their early lives and successes with a brief bio, but I encourage you to study them more in depth if you enjoy what they say and it resonates with you. These leaders have countless lessons to offer, but I highlight 10+ quotes, followed by how I interpret what they said based on my background and experiences. Since we are all unique and have different perspectives, you may interpret their quote in a different way, and that's perfectly okay.

The leaders featured in this book have added to my life immensely and I hope that this book will add to yours. If any of these quotes speak to your soul, I recommend you write them out on 3x5 notecards and hang them on your bathroom mirror, around your house, and at your office. Keep them as a constant reminder of what you need to do to take care of yourself and your mindset.

Most of these leaders have books, videos, and audiobooks, so I encourage you to give yourself the gift of spiritual development and invest time into learning from someone other than yourself. I'm excited about what you will discover about yourself and how you will use it to expand what's possible for you.

He Will Never Leave You or Forsake You

Many people think they have to clean up their lives and become pristine and perfect before they come to God. That is not the case at all. He will take you with all of your ugliness, darkness, and dysfunctions. The more broken the better. That way you'll know who healed you.

I denied God existed for 20 years. If He could forgive me and then heal me in order to serve others, He can certainly do the same for you. If you want to get closer to God, just ask. He's there, waiting for you to make the decision.

Am I perfect? Absolutely not!

Do I do everything right every single day? Nope!

Am I better than I used to be? Yes.

Have my broken places been healed and now I'm able to assist others with healing theirs? Yes.

Is this book relevant to everyone? No, it's not. This book is for those who are ready and can receive what I'm sharing. That's the beauty of our differences. I'm not meant to reach EVERYONE in the world. Just those that understand and care about what's shared.

Luke 22:32 (KJV) - But I have prayed for thee, that thy faith fail not: and when thou art converted, strengthen thy brethren.

Chapter 1

Bishop TD Jakes

I first saw Bishop TD Jakes when he was hosted by Joel Osteen at Lakewood Church. His sermon "The Outsider" in May 2014, made me sit up and pay attention. At that moment, I was ready to receive what he shared, and I started watching his videos.

Since then I've watched hundreds of videos featuring TD Jakes on YouTube and by streaming his live services. I've watched some of his messages three to six times if he's addressing an issue I'm having challenges with. What I love about him is he talks about the challenges that life throws at you, how to survive them and how to dig yourself out of the ditch you may be in. Mainly, how to survive the process of Becoming.

I have several journals with notes I've taken from TD Jakes and when my friends are having challenges, I send them relevant videos, based on where they are in the process. I attribute staying on the road to destiny to TD Jakes and the information that he's shared with millions of people around the world. I'm eternally grateful for him and the gifts he offers the world.

*Thomas Dexter (TD) Jakes was born in 1957 and grew up in West Virginia. He spent his teenage years working in local industries and caring for his father, who was on dialysis. His father owned a cleaning company and his mother was a teacher. He enrolled in college but dropped out.

He started preaching in a storefront church with 10 members, that he drove 1.5 hours to get to. Over the next 20 years, his congregation grew to 100 and then to 300. He preached the gospel in obscurity and without a lot of money. He eventually earned his degrees, completing a B. A. and M.A., and a Doctor of Ministry in Religious Studies.

TD Jakes has openly shared some of the hardships he endured during that 20-year period, which included not having enough money to keep all his utilities on at the same time. When he had lights, he didn't have water. If he had water, he didn't have gas. When his water was off, sometimes he would get water from his mom's house and his wife would warm it up so he and their kids could take a bath. He also shared that he couldn't afford pampers when his twin sons were born, so they used paper towel and duct tape. He shared that his car had a hole in the floorboard, and he covered it with cardboard.

Through the trials and the tests, he continued on his journey and eventually moved to Dallas with his wife, First Lady Serita Jakes, and five children. He started The Potters House and over the past 20 years, his congregation has grown to over 30,000 members. Giving back to his community and other impoverished areas, his ministries include a program for the homeless, incarcerated people, literacy programs, youth ministries, weight-loss programs, and mentoring and job-training programs. He also has clean water initiatives and educational programs in Africa.

TD Jakes has been awarded 13 honorary degrees and doctorates. He's been the spiritual counsel for the past four U. S. Presidents and has dined with Kings and Prime Ministers all over the world. He's published nearly 50 books (many of them *New York Times* bestsellers), produced 9 movies, and was awarded a Grammy for "Best Gospel or Chorus Album" in 2003. He is the first spiritual leader to have a daytime talk show, the "TD Jakes Show," which airs on OWN (Oprah Winfrey Network) and is syndicated around the world.
******

You are supposed to go through a period where people hate you, and attack you and throw rocks at you because you are not eligible to lead until you are eligible to duck.

Most people who have achieved high levels of success have people who don't like them as they ascend the ladder. This is evident for successful people across a multitude of industries.

People call NFL players "privileged," while failing to recognize that while they were at home on the couch as teenagers, these men were practicing in the scorching heat or blistering cold. People deplore pastors with mega churches but aren't willing to do one ounce of research to see that most of them had very meager and humble beginnings.

The rise in technology has created a proliferation of people who are angry and judgmental towards highly successful people. Successful people are also criticized and misunderstood by their coworkers, bosses and often those who are closest to them - their family and friends.

Not understanding that nearly every person who has achieved high levels of success has the exact same challenge creates pain, resentment, guilt and pressure. If you understand this is a common challenge for leaders, then you will know that you are in good company and it should take away some of the sting from the pain you feel.

Good leaders are great leaders because they pay attention to small details. They care about the little things.

Good leaders focus on 98 percent and do just enough to be good enough. Great leaders have incredible attention to detail and put their attention into the last two percent. Great leaders go the extra mile and focus on the little details and little things that often bring about the greatest result. This can be remembering to celebrate the occasions of their coworkers or personnel. Getting someone a cake for their birthday, bringing baked goods to the office for people to share, or visiting someone in the hospital.

It can also include making sure documents have been read and re-read for errors and being highly detailed and descriptive in tasks, rather than offering useless information. They have high grooming standards, making sure their shoes are always shined, suits tailored, and hair neatly trimmed.

When you go the extra mile and pay attention to the small things, it automatically sets you apart from everyone else. When you are set apart, higher level leaders will notice you and increased levels of promotion and recognition are inevitable.

When people haven't been through what you've been through, they have the tendency not to be so sensitive. Their advice is corrupted with the arrogance of their inexperience.

A few years ago, I read an article that criticized high achieving women. The author was very antagonistic, saying that we were mean, caddy, treated our counterparts as enemies and were martyrs. Angered by her comments, I quickly looked at her profile and saw that she had not achieved the same level of success of the women she criticized. In fact, she had only been employed for a few years and then became a women's leadership coach, sharing her "expertise" of what it takes for women to be successful.

If someone has not attained your level of success, they may be highly critical of you and what you've achieved. Be careful who you get your insight from and if someone has not achieved your level of success, they won't share the same battle scars that you have. Don't allow their uninformed opinions and judgments to hurt you and make you feel differently about yourself.

The first time you break out of what people expect you to be, don't expect them to celebrate.

As you look to break out of the norm and do something different, there will be resistance. Whether it's resistance from being the first person in your family to go to college or the first one to move away from your hometown, everyone will not support you. As you enter the workforce and start to ascend the ladder, you become competition and a threat to some people and they will not like it. Some will try to stop you. When you want to leave your job and become an entrepreneur, again, there will be resistance.

Highly successful people know that when you are going after new goals and are looking to disturb comfort zones and traditions, there will be silence. You can't work for applause,

4

gratitude or live for the support of others. If you do, you will be set up for great disappointment, because as you go higher and higher, the sound of silence and people supporting you is deafening.

Choose to step in a higher circle of influence and associate with people who are greater than you. They will not be threatened by your desire to become more and will assist you with Becoming who you were always meant to be.

I would rather learn how to hunt in the wild, rather than how to eat in captivity.

Most people around the world hate their jobs. This has been documented in countless polls and assessments. Why would you live 8-12 hours of your life every day in misery? After asking several people that question, they often cite a host of reasons to include financial considerations, houses, cars, lifestyle, etc. However, the most common reason is F-E-A-R. Fear of the unknown. Fear of starting over. Fear of not knowing how they will pay their bills.

Many people often say, "Golden Handcuffs." Getting paid too much money to leave a job they hate. They have settled to eat in a cage, rather than explore new territory. Have you succumbed to Golden Handcuffs and stay at a job that you hate, because of the fear of the unknown? People are dying at their desks and of boredom, but are too afraid to step out and take greater risks. Life is risky, but so is driving to and from work.

There are traffic accidents all over the country every single day, and people die driving to jobs they dislike. This tragedy is so common, that commuters are more worried about being late to work since traffic is backed up, than realizing that someone lost their life and won't be returning home to their families. You think freeing yourself to live the life you desire is risky? It may be time to shift your perspective on risk.

Do you know that you've allowed other people to put so much on you that you don't know who you are?

This is a common issue that leaders have. Leaders are not only leaders at work, but we are also leaders in our families, community, and other areas of our life. As we continue to ascend, we create alliances, partnerships, relationships and friendships with others. Leaders will ensure that the needs of others are taken care of before our own.

The challenge with this scenario comes when you find yourself shrinking, conforming and adjusting who you are to fit in at work, in relationships and friendships. Over time, after adjusting to suit the needs of so many people, you can lose sight of who you are at your core. Losing your sense of self and authenticity to fit it. You stop living to make yourself happy and instead sacrifice your happiness and desires to make other people happy. This is draining.

Most people think it's selfish to think about themselves and what they really want in life. You know the needs of others and what would make them happy, but rarely stop to ask yourself, what would make you happy. Give that question some thought and take the necessary steps to make it happen.

You got more degrees than a thermometer. You got more titles than they can put on a business card, and you are still dysfunctional. The reason is, you have put your energy into your image and left your reality unchanged.

Are you only seeking to look whole on the outside and using makeup, perfume, cars, clothes and external things to mask your inner pain and distorted view of yourself? You can put a dress and lipstick on a skunk, but it will still stink.

Only by working on how you feel about yourself, will you be able to create real change in your life.

Psalm 51:10 (NIV) says, "Create in me a pure heart, O God, and renew a steadfast spirit within me."

6

Focus on creating a clean heart by forgiving yourself and others, and your perspective of self will change internally. That's where it counts the most.

What a tragedy to waste your days being important when you could have just been happy.

As a leader and someone who's highly visible in your office, community or industry, you start to play a role. It's easy to think that people are watching your every move, especially the people that are waiting for you to fail. Adding a security clearance to the mix or having a job where your after-work activities can greatly affect your position, creates additional paranoia.

Living this way is almost as if you are a walking mannequin. A plastic figure who is solely focused on how you look at all times, with a puffed out ego, but without any tangible feelings. There is a new trend going around called, "The Mannequin Challenge." It's not new. People have been playing this game in their real lives for years.

For the most part, this paranoia and mental condition are self-inflicted and most of the people you think are watching you, are too busy worrying about what they look like. They aren't paying any attention to you. Relax and work on unlayering who you want everyone to think you are and Become who you truly are. Authenticity is a gift and will set you FREE!

When you are feeding more people than people are feeding you, it creates pressure.

In my previous career, I had 160 people working for me and mentored an additional 70 people outside of my office. Yet, I only had 10 mentors. Some may say that 10 mentors is a high number, but they were necessary since I was a high achiever. They all had different perspectives on my challenges based on their backgrounds and experience. Regardless, with 10 people feeding me as I fed over 230 people, there was bound to be an imbalance and burnout.

As a leader, how many people are you mentoring, responsible for and are depending on you for inspiration? If the number that you're feeding is significantly larger than those feeding you, is it any surprise you're overwhelmed?

Work to right the balance by choosing to mentor in a group setting rather than one on one. Start to qualify your mentees for getting your time. Are they still complaining about the same issue months after you assisted them with it? If so, reduce your interactions with the ones that are wasting your time, and focus on those who immediately implement your recommendations.

Finding your destiny will always disappoint people who have appointed you to theirs.

When you tell people your dreams and what God has placed in your heart, do they try to talk you out of it or speak fear into you? People who have attached what you can do for them and how they will get ahead with your input, don't want you getting any bright ideas that will exclude them. They will not and I repeat, **WILL NOT** support you in your vision. Be ready for it and know that you must leave them behind to pursue your destiny.

It is your purpose and unknowingly it has become your goal to live out the damnation of the words you rehearse to yourself.

What is the story that plays in your head or the story that you repeat to others when you feel like you can't move forward?

"He won't let me." "What if I fail?" "I'm broke." "I was abused as a child." "I'm stupid." "No one will listen to me." "It's too late."

When you say these things over and over again, you're actually living out the words you're speaking. Nothing that has happened to you in your past can stop you from moving forward today. You are letting words bind you down to wretchedness and shame, and not taking massive action to break your self-imposed limitations. How can words **physically** hold you back and stop you from moving forward? They can't. Go NOW in the direction of your dreams!!

We are always tormented by vision. It's a painful thing to be a visionary because a visionary sees what shall be and wakes up to deal with what is.

Visionaries always live in the reality of what they see in their dreams and what will be instead of living in what is. It's tough to be a visionary because your physical circumstances can be terrible, but you still keep a smile on your face knowing that one day your vision will come to pass. It takes discipline, constant action, and FAITH! But one day, the dream of your heart will be realized. Don't give up!

Some of your friends are hitmen sent from hell to take you back. They make you feel bad for wanting to do better. They don't like you because you wanted out of what they were into and they are determined to convince you that there is no other world but the world they created.

This is pretty self-explanatory. If you know this to be true, what will you do? How will you manage the circle you're rolling with? Is it time to get a new circle?

**If you want to get clarity on who your real friends are and the ones you need to leave behind, get access to my FREE course, Take Inventory at www.christyrutherford.com/takeinventory

Chapter 2

Joel Osteen

As I shared earlier, I started watching Pastor Joel Osteen in 2009. As I switched through the channels over the years, I often saw him, noticed his hair, southern accent, and smile, but didn't watch him. In 2009, I was evolving and wanted to get closer to God and although I was attending a church at the time, I didn't feel comfortable there. While traveling to San Francisco, I found myself feeling guilty one Sunday because I wasn't in church. I saw him on the television that day, and never stopped watching.

What I love about Joel Osteen is that he shares information on **expecting** God to show up in your life and provide you with greater things. He talks about **expecting** explosive and accelerated blessings and **expecting** something good to happen to you. He also shares insight about **expecting** people to be good to you.

It's living your life from a different perspective and **expecting** great things, as opposed to just letting life happen. I attribute him to being someone that saved me from myself and self-defeat during that challenging time in my life. I considered him and the spirit of his church to be like heart defibrillators, and he jumpstarted my heart every time I thought I coded. He has amazing messages to share and impacts millions of people around the world. I'm so grateful for him.

*Joel Osteen was born in 1963 in Houston, Texas. His father John Osteen was the pastor of Lakewood Church. He went to college in Oklahoma for a year, but returned home and urged his parents to set up a television ministry for the church.

For 17 years, Joel Osteen was behind the scenes as a cameraman and traveled all over the world with his father. He would go to his father's house on Saturday night and pick out his suit and tie to wear the following day. After his father's hair and makeup person moved, he asked Victoria (Joel's wife), to start doing it for him. In an effort to serve, she agreed and continued to do his hair and makeup for over 10 years. His father always encouraged him to deliver a sermon or speak during the church services, but as an introvert, who was low key and shy, he always declined and felt more comfortable behind the scenes.

In 1999, when his father experienced kidney failure, he asked Joel Osteen to step up and speak. He finally agreed and delivered his first sermon to nearly 6,000 people, wearing a pair of his father's shoes for emotional support. The following week, his father had a heart attack and died. Joel Osteen's first sermon was the last sermon his father heard.

Joel and Victoria Osteen were thrust into leadership of the church and within a year, the church grew from nearly 5,000 people to over 28,000. In 2001, Forbes magazine noted that Lakewood had grown into the largest non-denominational church in the U.S. In 2003, after years of legal battles, Lakewood acquired the Compaq Center, which was the home of the NBA team Houston Rockets. Since then, Lakewood has more than 45,000 weekly attendees.

Joel and Victoria Osteen's ministry is impacting people all over the world through live services, televised, live stream and recorded online church services. They reach every U.S. television market and over 100 nations around the world. In 2014, "Joel Osteen Radio" was launched on Sirius XM; a channel dedicated to the inspirational messages of Joel and Victoria. Their "Night of Hope" events have hosted over two million people across the U.S. and around the world.

He's written 7 *New York Times* bestsellers and his first book, *Your Best Life Now,* remained a bestseller for more than 200 weeks. Their ministry programs include feeding the hungry, providing vaccinations, delivering medical supplies, working with abandoned baby centers and working with centers for troubled teens. They've also renovated, built libraries and technology rooms at a large number of schools in impoverished areas in Houston.

Joel Osteen's brother Paul, is a surgeon and travels to Africa several months a year to operate on people in remote villages, who otherwise wouldn't be provided that level of care. Joel and Victoria Osteen have two children that perform as a part of the music ministry, which regularly releases music on Itunes.

(source JoelOsteen.com)

******

Sometimes God will tell us to do things we're afraid of. Get out of your comfort zone and do it afraid.

When God places a vision in your heart, it will be big and will blow your mind. You may not feel like you're the right person that will be able to manage what you've seen and that may be true. You are the right person physically, but you need to BECOME the right person spiritually in order be the person that will own the vision.

You have everything that you need to Become who you were meant to be. Continue to move forward, take action, serve others and your path will continue to unfold. It's okay to be afraid. Do it anyway!

To get to your destiny, you have to pass the small tests.

If you are walking with God or want to strengthen your relationship, how are you demonstrating your knowledge? You can wear a gold cross that weighs 50 pounds, quote the book of Matthew or praise dance until you wear the soles off your shoes, but if you don't show kindness to others, how are you demonstrating God's love?

Look for ways to be good to people. Hold the door open for them, even if they're far away. Offer to take a person's cart back to the store if you are walking that way or go out of your way to assist them. Help an elderly person get something off a shelf or load their groceries into their car. Buy a cup of coffee for the coworker that says nasty things about you.

Find ways to demonstrate the love of God and others will be able to see that you're a person of faith by what you do and not what you say.

In life, there are always two voices vying for your attention. The voice of faith and the voice of defeat.

When you have the choice to step out and do something different, do you talk yourself out of it before you even get started? Do you feel like you need more money, information, or time before you can begin? With two voices in your head fighting for attention, when you learn how to tame the negative one, your life will take on a whole new meaning.

Hebrews 11:1 (KJV) - Now faith is the substance of things hoped for, the evidence of things not seen.

As you look to defeat the negative voice, sometimes you have to be your own voice of faith. You need to speak the things you desire in your life out loud until they show up because when God asks you to move, it's time to move. That's working with applied faith.

Life is too short to hang around people who are not making you better. Who are not pushing you forward. You don't have time to waste with people that are causing you to compromise, draining your energy, getting you off course negative, critical, bitter, jealous people. Your destiny is calling. You have an assignment to fulfill.

Show me your friends and I'll show you your future. Chickens flock together on the ground and eagles soar alone. Chickens also eat their own crap. When you're walking towards your destiny, you don't have time for stinky breath chickens....ah hem, I mean, you don't have time for people and their negative comments. Leave the chickens alone and soar into the direction of your dreams!! You have an assignment to fulfill!

There are times you have to lose something to gain something to go to the next level.

What are you willing to give up to get to the next level? Many people complain that they don't have enough time to work on their dreams, but they don't miss a football or basketball game. Some people say they don't have enough money to finance their business idea, but drive a luxury car, live in a huge house, eat out regularly, drink gourmet coffee and never miss a concert or movie.

In order to get something different, you are going to have to sacrifice something. If you aren't willing to give up the comforts of your current lifestyle to take the necessary steps to get a greater lifestyle, do you really deserve it? Are you willing to give up a good life for a great life? That decision rests solely with you. What are you going to do?

Don't use your energy to worry, use it to believe.

It takes just as much energy to worry as it does to believe. You can spend five minutes worrying about everything that can go wrong or you can spend five minutes reading a book, watching a video or taking some type of action that will move you closer to what you desire. We all have 24 hours in a day. How are you using yours?

Declare, "Something good is going to happen to me today."

I remember hearing Joel Osteen say this nearly six years ago. My life was good, but I wanted it to be better. I wanted to be happier and have less drama. I expected drama to happen on a regular basis and I was not disappointed. I typed this quote out in big letters, put a picture of some flowers around it and hung it on my door.

As I left the house every day, I knew that I had a choice to determine how my day was going to go. When I went to work, was I expecting chaos or could I expect for something good to happen? This simple exercise magically shifted things in my life. Today, I have this on the mirror in my bathroom, along with 30 other quotes, so I can see them immediately after waking up, before going to bed and several times during the day. Will you give it a shot and see how your life will change for the best?

**To keep positive information in front of you at all times, get my 12 favorite quotes (cutouts) that you can hang around your home or office at www.christyrutherford.com/quotes

When your vision is negative, your life will follow that path. Life is not going to change until you change the picture.

What do you spend most of your time daydreaming about? Everything that you've done wrong in life? Reliving the way that people mistreated you? Thinking about what someone said that hurt your feelings?

What you think about and what you visualize is how your life will play out. You are the writer, director, producer and leading actor/actress in your life. What type of movie are you producing? If you feel stuck and like you are going in circles, it's because you're focused on your past and not your future. Throw away that script and create a new one TODAY!

Don't let what was once a miracle become ordinary.

I've often said that we miss today's miracle by praying for tomorrow's desire. What did you ask God for five years ago? What did you fight for and work for and then celebrate when it showed up? Was it a new house? A husband/wife? A baby?

How do you feel about that miracle now? Are you constantly complaining about how dirty the house gets and all the work you have to do to keep it well maintained? Does your spouse get on your nerves and you wish they would evaporate out of your life? Is your kid throwing tantrums or stopping you from getting quality sleep?

Can you remember what you felt like when you had a strong longing for those things to come into your life? Every time you're frustrated with what once brought you so much joy, stop, take a few deep breaths and then give gratitude. Don't let your miracles become ordinary.

Maybe it's time for them to be unhappy. If they get mad, they are not a friend, they are manipulators.

So many people live in bondage because they don't want to make their "friends" upset or mad. Real friends won't allow you to sacrifice your happiness for theirs or continue to use you for what you can do for them. Real friends won't run you in the ground with their requests or constantly ask you for money and not pay you back. It's time to get real clear about who you have in your circle and who you call F-R-I-E-N-D.

Don't let them put limitations on you and convince you that you can't accomplish your dreams. Sometimes because of their own issues that they're not dealing with, their own insecurities, they'll try to push you down, hold you down, so they don't look bad.

Sometimes people will guilt you into doing something that you don't want to do so they don't look bad. They don't want you to step out on your dreams because if you fail, it will make the family look bad. Or it will make your circle of friends doubt your true ability.

Some family members will hold you hostage in toxic relationships, because of the aesthetics of it. A doctor married to a lawyer. A high level government worker married to a professor. You look good together and smile in public, but you are both dead on the inside.

Don't let the expectations of others hold you hostage to a life you don't want. If they are worried about how *their image* will be affected when *you* make a decision for *your* life, you need to drop them and run! This may also include family until they get over themselves.

Chapter 3

Paulo Coelho

A few years ago, I picked up *The Alchemist* and couldn't put it down. I finished it in less than three days and then read it again. After that, I took extensive notes. It's an AMAZING book. Last year, I read *Manuscript Found in Accra* and again, finished it in less than two days. I immediately bought the audiobook, because I want the words from the book to become a part of my natural language. I've heard it over 50 times...okay, more like 100.

Paulo Coelho has a way of writing that will speak to your soul. I'm not sure how he's able to tell the story of a spiritual journey that feels like my own personal story, but his writings are treasured by millions of people around the world. I highly recommend all of his books, but the two mentioned above are ones you must add to your library. It's hard to limit his quotes to just 10. All of these are from the *Manuscript Found in Accra,* a GEM and spiritual offering to mankind. It will melt your heart and ignite your spirit.

*Author Paulo Coelho was born in Rio de Janeiro, Brazil in 1947. He attended Jesuit schools and was raised by devout Catholic parents. Early in his life, he wanted to be a writer but was discouraged by his parents, who saw no future in that profession in Brazil. His rebellious behavior made them commit him to a mental asylum 3 times, starting when he was 17.

"I have forgiven," he said. "It happens with love, all the time - when you have this love towards someone else, but you want this person to change, to be like you. And then love can be very destructive."

Coelho eventually got out and enrolled in law school, but dropped out to indulge in the "sex, drugs and rock 'n' roll" of hippie life in the 1970s. Protesting the country's military rule, he wrote lyrics for Brazilian musicians and was jailed three times for his political activism. He was subjected to torture while in prison.

After drifting in several professions, at age 36, Coelho walked more than 500 miles along the Road to Santiago de Compostela, a site of Catholic pilgrimage. He had a spiritual awakening during the walk and eventually quit his other jobs to devote himself full-time to the craft of writing.

In 1987, he wrote *The Alchemist* in two weeks, but it took several years for the book to take off. Through a series of events, the book gained notoriety and became a worldwide phenomenon, selling nearly 35 million copies. It's the most translated book in the world by any living author. He's written 26 books (many of them *New York Times* bestsellers) and sold more than 65 million copies in at least 59 languages.

Paulo Coelho's been married to his wife, Christina Oiticica since 1980. (source Biography.com)

******

Many of us believe that we will hurt those we love if we leave behind everything in the name of our dreams. But those who truly want the best for us want us to be happy, even if they can't understand what we are doing and even if, at first, they try to stop us from going ahead by means of threats, promises and tears.

Just like the seasons change, there will be people in your life for a season and very few for a lifetime. When friendships and relationships become toxic and you feel like you are being held back and choked out, it's time to let them go.

A key phrase of when it's time to leave, is when people ask, "Who do you think you are?"

This applies to your friends and coworkers. Don't allow others to impose their limitations and fears on you. The leaves on trees dry up and fall away in the fall, but a new set comes fresh and anew in spring. Make room for new friendships and experiences by cutting away the old. Only then will you see what you are really capable of achieving.

Your enemies are not the adversaries who were put there to test your courage. They are the cowards who were put there to test your weakness.

How easy is it for someone to set you off and make you angry? How often do you give away your joy to people who aren't worth your time or energy? Not reacting to the negativity of others takes strength and discipline. Discipline allows you to stay calm in the midst of chaos.

When you are easily provoked and manipulated, anyone can make you a victim. If someone sets you off regularly, you're displaying your weakness to them. Choose to manage your negative reactions to negative people. Rise above the challenge and respond accordingly.

The wounded person should ask himself: "Is it worth filling my heart with hatred and dragging the weight of it around with me?"

Did you know that holding on to what someone did to you in the past stops you from moving forward? Did you know that it's like being anchored to one spot and not being able to move? Knowing this, who do you need to forgive?

Are you willing to let go of the baggage, the scenarios and the people that are stopping you from living the life you desire? It's a simple as CHOOSING your bright and expansive future over a dark and crappy past.

Most people have a problem with forgiving others because they think it lets the other person off the hook for what they did. Forgiveness has absolutely nothing to do with the other person. They don't need to know (nor do they care) that you are forgiving them. It's a choice that you have to make in order to live the life that you desire.

You will see that you are about to arrive at a place where very few have ever set foot, and you will think that you don't deserve what life is giving you. You will forget all the obstacles you overcame, all that you suffered and sacrificed.

And because of that feeling of guilt, you could unconsciously destroy everything that took you so long to build.

Have you achieved high levels of success and somehow feel guilty about living your lifestyle when people in your family don't have as much? Have you achieved success, but because of the tradeoffs you made, you don't feel successful? Do you lack self-confidence, because you don't feel like you deserve to be where you are?

Regardless of the reason, you should celebrate when you break the chains of normalcy and set new standards. Even if you have to celebrate alone, make sure you take ownership of your greatness and don't let others steal the joy of high achievement. You earned it!

Difficulty is the name of an ancient tool that was created purely to help us define who we are.

The greatest times of growth and development occur during challenging times. When times are hard, it makes you look for new and creative ways to resolve them. Stand in the face of challenges and work hard! Do whatever it takes to overcome the obstacles in your path and you will be a better person. It will also show you what you are truly made of.

How you respond to challenges also highlights your weak spots. Identify them and work to become stronger in those areas. What are your challenges showing you?

Avoid those who talk a great deal before acting, those who never take a step without being quite sure that it will bring them respect.

There are talkers and then there are doers. You've seen them. The people who always TALK about what they're going to do, but never take ACTION. They've been telling the same story over and over again, about how they are going to change or will do something different with their life. How long will you allow them to waste your time?

People who never take action without being sure it will bring them respect aren't risk takers. They're not looking to achieve excellence. Great leaders and visionaries are misunderstood for a time, and waiting for respect or approval is not an option for them. Get around people that make you feel alive and leave the non-action talkers where they are.

Help us to see in each grain of desert sand proof of the miracle of difference, and may that encourage us to accept ourselves as we are. Because just as no two grains of sand are alike, so no two humans beings will think and act in the same way.
Wanting to fit in and be liked by others has created a society of conformists. People are getting plastic surgery to look like celebrities, hoping they will somehow feel like them too. They don't. We are all created unique and different for a reason. We are not meant to be the same or want the same things.
What makes you feel weird, is your greatness unrealized. Embrace your weirdness. Explore it, nurture it and grow it until you see the hidden gem within it. Then multiply your efforts to develop it and take ownership of it. Embracing who you are and your uniqueness will set your soul on fire. Do it and watch the whole world come to see you burn!

Help us to awaken the Love sleeping within us before we awaken Love in other people. Only then will we be able to attract affection, enthusiasm and respect.
Ahhhh love. What is love and why is it elusive for some people? Do you feel loveable? I've found that the greatest challenge that people have in love is actually loving themselves. If you don't love yourself, no amount of love that someone gives you will be enough to fill the gaping hole you have in your life.
Sometimes the person that you are waiting on to show up and give love meaning for you is Y-O-U. Do the work on yourself to clean your heart, strengthen your character and you'll love

yourself more. Only then can you really attract and maintain a healthy and fulfilling relationship with someone else.

Scars are medals branded on the flesh and your enemies will be frightened by them because they are proof of your long experience of battle.

If you've lived long enough and have achieved any level of success, then you've fought a battle to get there. Whether you were criticized from your family, your friends turned their back on you, toxic relationships or bad bosses, you have scars. How you feel about those scars is up to you.

Do they cause you pain and serve as a reminder of what you went through? Or, do you look at them and celebrate them as obstacles you've overcome to achieve greatness?

Be willing to view your scars in a different light and celebrate them. Then your enemies will truly be frightened, because you are wearing them as a Warrior and not as a victim.

What is success? It is being able to go to bed each night with your soul at peace.

Do you have all that you desire financially and materially, but don't have inner peace? You may have a bigger house and better car, but they also come with more responsibility and volatility if you lose your job. This can cause unrest. High achievement also means you spend more time at work, and less time with your family and friends. The guilt from missing out on important days with your family can also cause unrest. As a leader, you have to manage different personalities with your employees and bosses, which can create additional unrest.

If you are stressed out and overwhelmed with the responsibilities of being you, what are you doing about it? Are you really successful if you don't sleep well at night worrying about a multitude of issues?

Consider incorporating meditation into your daily routine. Five minutes will make a considerable difference in the clarity you'll have during the day and how you sleep at night.

Meditation not only lowers your blood pressure, but it can also amp up your immune system, while improving your ability to concentrate.

There are tons of meditation apps and videos on YouTube. Give chanting or Om's a try to vibrate the negative energy off you. It takes time to train your mind to slow down, so be patient. If you can't sit in silence, try guided meditations. My favorite meditation app is called, Relax and Rest (green face logo). Get the paid version and set yourself free!

Chapter 4

Joyce Meyer

The first time I tried to watch Pastor Joyce Meyer I couldn't do it because I felt that her personality was slightly abrasive. Years later, I learned that what we don't like in others is typically a reflection of who we are. After she was hosted by Joel Osteen several times, I discovered that we were a lot alike. She's straight forward, direct and uses personal stories from her life and her walk with God motivate and inspire others.

My lack of self-awareness affected how I saw her. She didn't change, I did. Isn't that an epiphany that will change your life??!! I love Joyce Meyer and the stories she shares are so relatable and funny as you see yourself in the things she's done. I'm now playing catch up on all the great insights she's shared over the past 30 years.

*Joyce Meyer was born in 1943 in St. Louis. When she was a little girl, her father sexually abused her and continued to do so for 15 years. She said that her mom knew, but was too afraid to do anything about it. She confided in her aunt and uncle and they also declined to step in and do something.

She got married at 19 years old to get out of her family's house. Her husband cheated on her regularly and they ended up divorcing within five years. She later met Dave Meyer and they were married. Joyce Meyer shares humorous stories about her walk with God and all the ways he unraveled who she was. She openly talks about her past and dysfunctions and connects with people in a way that others aren't able to because they only want to share the whole parts of their character.

She shared that later in her father's life, he apologized for sexually abusing her and told her that he didn't know how much he hurt her growing up. She then asked him if he wanted to be saved, and he agreed. That day he gave his life to God.

Joyce Meyer has authored nearly 100 books, (many of them *New York Times* bestsellers), which have been translated into 100 languages. She's distributed more than 12 million books around the world free of charge and sells millions of copies yearly. She hosts nearly 12 domestic and international conferences every year, teaching people to enjoy their everyday lives. For 30 years, her annual women's conference has attracted over 200,000 women from around the world. She also hosts a TV and radio show, Enjoying Everyday Life®, which broadcasts to an audience of nearly 4.5 billion people worldwide. (source JoyceMeyer.org)
******

I honestly believe that it's much better to step out and find out, than to stay hidden in a closet all your life and wonder.

When you want to go after your dreams, do you think you're going to fail? How do you know that's true? If you think you're going to fail, then you likely will, but if you commit to giving it everything you got, at least you failed while going towards a worthwhile goal.

Failure will teach you what you didn't know about yourself, other people and your vision. Dust yourself off and go at it again with the new information. Don't wait until you're on your death bed and wonder what you coulda', woulda', shoulda'. Don't take your limited time here for granted. Go NOW!!

A lot of people have a gift that will take them somewhere, but not enough character to keep them there when they get there.

How many successful people have you seen crash and burn over the past five years because they did or said something that caused a fire storm? Some celebrities have had their entire careers burned to the ground in a matter of weeks, because they said something racist or negative, or were caught on camera acting in a manner outside of good moral standard (in alignment with their public persona).

Some survived the storm, others didn't. As you're walking towards your destiny, know that God will not release you fully until you've developed the character and necessary traits that will keep you where you're going. Respect the process and know that God is keeping track of you passing the small tests. If you can do the right things consistently in obscurity, then you can be trusted to do the right when you have the spotlight.

There are dreamers who don't work and workers that don't dream, and neither one of them work.

James 24:17 (NIV) says, "...faith by itself, if it is not accompanied by action, is dead."

Proverbs 29:18 (NIV) says, "Where there is no *vision*, the *people perish.*"

You need to dream about what you want and work. It should also be connected to a larger vision than just wanting to make money. The thought of wanting money will only take you so far. What do you want to do with the money and how will you use it to better the lives of others?

Do you want to rebuild your church, build a school, community center, orphanage or feed the homeless? Your vision should be attached to the betterment of mankind and the human condition. Dream a bigger dream to serve others and work towards it every single day.

Nobody is truly free until they no longer have a need to impress people.

When you get ready to buy something or as you're getting dressed to go out, are your decisions influenced by how other people will feel about it? Do you buy an expensive purse or watch, so others will see it and think you're successful? Do you buy an expensive suit or dress and then opt to wear it somewhere when you want to stand out in the crowd as someone who has money?

There's nothing wrong with wanting nice things and desiring to wear premium clothing. The problem is when you're doing it solely to impress others, because you're deriving your value from *what you have* and not *who you are*. Be mindful and take note of yourself when you may do this and figure out why.

People, you need to take care of yourself. Your body is the house you live in and if you destroy it, then you have to leave.
Are you working yourself into exhaustion at your job to provide for your family? Are you too busy to get enough sleep, eat the right foods and exercise regularly? One thing is for sure, if you don't take the time to do these things for yourself, you're accelerating your life into an early grave. Your body is your temple, make sure you treat it as such.
**For a self-assessment on the areas that you may need to address, get my free Work-Life Balance Assessment at www.christyrutherford.com/worklife

Don't give up your life just to make someone else happy, who in the end won't care.
Do you feel like people are using you for what you can do for them, but never show up when you need them? Are you miserable because every time your phone rings, it's someone asking you for your time, money or other resources?

How long has this been going on and how long will you continue to ALLOW it to happen? Yes, you are allowing it to happen! That means you have the power to stop it. Start saying no.

I've heard it said that 90 percent of your friends won't even come to your funeral. Yet, these are the people you are living your life for and allowing to control you. They run your life when you're afraid to be criticized by them and **they won't even come to your funeral!** I thought the saying was pretty funny, until I saw it play out in real life when one of my good friends died in a car accident.

We are all solely responsible for making ourselves happy. If you are surrendering your happiness to make someone else happy, it's time to stop. They are responsible for their happiness and if you've been working tirelessly for the past 5-10 years to make someone else happy and they're still miserable, then are they the real problem or is it you? If you are always playing the role of rescuer, it's time for you to rescue yourself! Make the choice to save yourself today.

Half of the stress that we go through is trying to pay for and take care of what we own.

I talked to a guy once who was the most miserable person I had met in a long time. After watching him in his misery over a few months, as a life coach, I couldn't take it anymore and had to ask what was going on. He told me that he hated his job. When I asked why he didn't consider leaving, since it made him so miserable, he said he couldn't leave because he had just bought his dream home. I then asked what seemed obvious to me, "Why not sell the house, get a smaller house and then switch jobs."

He looked at me like I had two heads and said, "It's my dream house!"

I left the conversation right there. The mortgage on his dream house had eaten up his disposable income, so he was no longer able to eat out as much or afford vacations. Worrying about paying for the mortgage on his dream house kept him up at night when the government shut down a few years ago. What do you have that's keeping you up at night and how long will you be a slave to what you own? Do you own it or does it own you?

We're always quick to judge people who have a problem in an area where we have strength.

Do you judge people for being overweight and unhealthy, because you exercise regularly and have a proper diet? Are you healthy physically, but suffer from depression, which makes you unhealthy mentally? Do you judge a person for having a broken marriage, when you're happily married, yet you have unruly kids?

The problem with judging others, is for every minute we spend looking at the problems of others, it leaves us one less minute to look at and address our own. No one is perfect and we're all dealing with something in our lives. Be kind to others and love them for who they are, faults and all, because you want others to love you for yours. You get back what you put out in the world.

You can get over a broken past if you decide to believe there is nothing in your past that will keep you from having a great future.

There is nothing in your past that can keep you from living the life you desire, even if you had a traumatic childhood. Are you choosing to live your life looking through the lenses of the wounded child? Shift your perspective and see that if you could survive that, it made you a stronger person.

If you had a felony in your past, do you walk around using that felony as a reason you can't get the job you desire? Be open to seeking entrepreneurial opportunities that only measure you based on results and not your past.

Are you driving your life's car looking through the wide and expansive windshield (future) or through the small rear view mirror (past)? If you drove your car and only used the rear view mirror, you would likely go 20 feet before you ended up in a ditch. If you feel like you're stuck, then it's time to start focusing on your future and drive looking at everything that's in front of you and leave your past behind. Everything that you want in life is waiting for you to do the work to claim it. Go NOW!!

One of the things you can do when you have a problem that you can't solve, is go be a blessing to somebody else.

When you're stuck in your mind and can't seem to move forward, go and help someone else. Serving others will free up space in your mind and will release energy from your heart. There's something magical in this statement because you'll find that the more you assist others, your problems will go away. Whether they were solved through serving or they don't seem like problems anymore. Give this a shot and you'll find that your life will change for the best.

Chapter 5

John Gray

I started watching Pastor John Gray when he joined Joel Osteen's church as the Associate Pastor four years ago. What I love about him is he shares insight on how to strengthen your walk with God, and he's hilarious. He's a comedian, singer and Pastor. He's also not shy about being vulnerable and sharing his challenges as he walks through them, giving the audience a sense that they are not alone in their challenges at that moment. John Gray is a powerful and gifted speaker and I watch his messages from Lakewood Church's live services page. He's also on YouTube.

*John W. Gray III., was born and raised in Cincinnati, Ohio. He's the product of two musically gifted parents, however, his father left his mom when he was a baby. One day, when he was less than five years old, he was sexually assaulted as he played outside in front of his home. He carried the resentment of that terrifying incident for an extended period of time, feeling that if his father was there, it wouldn't have happened.

John Gray went to college but returned home his sophomore year. He flunked out because he lost focus after a sudden and devastating illness of his beloved grandmother. Derailed temporarily, he enrolled at the local university and became a part of their traveling choir. He answered the call to preach on his 21st birthday and started preaching at a Baptist Church.

He later became a cast member in a touring stage play, starring Grammy Award-winning gospel artist Kirk Franklin and The Family. From directing, producing and co-producing award winning films, John Gray has released two musical albums, a comedy DVD and appeared on the hit television shows "Sister, Sister" and "Tyler Perry's The House of Payne." In July 2016, he starred in a talk show featured on Fox called The Preachers.

John Gray seamlessly integrates preaching, comedy, music, exhortation and encouragement into one package. He serves as an Associate Pastor at Lakewood Church in Houston, Texas under the leadership of Joel Osteen, with his wife Aventer and two young children.
******

Religious people will beat you up because you haven't changed at the pace of their will, but your salvation is a personal walk.

When seeking a relationship with God, it is a personal journey. Many people think that they have to wait until they get their life right before they seek a connection with God, but that's just the opposite. Seek a relationship with Him and over an extended period of time, your life will become better. Change and spiritual development is not an overnight process. It takes times to grow, develop and change into who you were meant to be.

Be patient with yourself and seek to be better each day. In time, your life will unfold in divine destiny. Don't allow other people to make you feel like you should change in a microwave minute. Your walk is a personal one. Keep it close to your heart and hold it sacred. Everyone doesn't need to know.

God is allowing us to walk through seasons of loss and longing in order to get us to admit what we sense deep inside, "Something is missing."

If you have an empty feeling regardless of what you've accomplished, you may be searching for significance. What will you be remembered for when you die? What impact did you make in the life of others? Did you live the life you wanted to live or have you allowed others to talk you out of it?

Consider reinvesting your time into activities that bring you the greatest joy. Get off early and volunteer with a cause close to your heart. Become a mentor or youth coach. Find ways to serve others and your heart will expand in ways you never imagined.

When you get healed in your heart, you'll realize that you are enough and whoever you are and whoever is called into your life will love the real you and not the projected image of you.

When you get a clean heart and FINALLY love yourself for who you are and your uniqueness, you'll no longer hide behind a mask of who others want you to be. **It is the greatest gift in the world!!!!**

Keep growing as Spiritual Coach Holly Nunan said in the Foreword and you'll Unbecome who you thought you were and reveal the you that's been there all along.

God forms a new man from the old man and there are times when the old man and new man will war against one another and you will think you are going crazy.

We are spiritual beings in a physical body. As you're walking out your destiny with God, it is a process of Becoming. Really, it's UN-becoming who you thought you were and revealing who you are meant to be. This transformation will set a person at war with themselves. It is sooooooo hard. You will only understand this if you are walking out your destiny or have walked it out. If you're in process now and think you're going nuts, you're on the right path. Keep moving forward!
**To get 20 of my favorite quotes (cutouts) that you can place around your house or office, go to
www.christyrutherford.com/freequotes

Some people are so busy chasing the illusion of success, that they miss the decay in their spirit.

What's the point of having it all if you feel like you're hollow on the inside? What's the point of having enough money to buy anything you want, if you have a nasty attitude or are on the brink of depression?

There are tradeoffs made on the upward ladder of success. Be mindful of what you're trading. If you feel like you've given up too much (your inner peace), do the work to get your joy back. This may mean leaving your career or taking a break. The time will be worth it if it saves your life. Some people die at their desk by working themselves into an early grave. They made a sacrifice, but it was the wrong one.

Work to get clarity on where you are today if your life doesn't look the way you thought it would. What do you have to give up to get it?

The day of your announcement is not always the same day of your anointing. The anointing is future-minded. The announcement is present-minded. So He will anoint you for a thing you're not ready to occupy and He will allow the process of life to prune out of you anything that will hinder the anointing from flowing later.

We are all meant to contribute our gifts and greatness to the world. However, only a few people will answer the call. Fewer people will take the first step and only a very small number of people will finish the walk. Those are the people you see that have impacted the world, President Obama, Steve Jobs, Oprah, Elon Musk, Howard Shultz, etc.

When they got the vision in their hearts, they weren't successful overnight. It took time…lots of time, work, collaboration, faith, failure, persistence and a whole host of things in order to bring the vision to pass. What separates them from the people who die with their dreams unfulfilled is ACTION.

Everybody's got a storm in their life, some folk just hide their umbrella better.

Everybody is going through something. EVERYBODY!!!! From the CEO to the janitor, to the single mom, to the working mom, to the stay at home mom, to the cashier, to the cook, to the parking attendant, to the doorman, to the postal worker, to the fireman, to the person living in the projects, to the billionaire. EVERYBODY!!

Knowing this, be mindful of your actions and choose to be kind to others. You never know how what you say to them will affect their day and how they see themselves. Make sure it's in a positive way.

God allows storms to expel unnecessary people, to extract the anointing from your life and to eliminate unnecessary relationships.

I asked God once, "Will I have ANY friends left when this thing is over??" It seems like nearly everyone I had in my life vanished, turned on me or said negative things about me as I chose to walk out my destiny. In reality, it's all a part of the process.

There are people that come into our lives and they aren't meant to stay forever. There are people who are serving your present and those that will get you to your destiny. There are also people who speak fear into you and those who speak faith.

After redefining what success meant to me, I no longer needed people to buy me drinks and listen to my woe-is-me stories as I talked about all the things that were going wrong in my life. I needed friends who supported the vision I had in my heart; as big and outrageous as it may seem.

I offer this to say that everyone will not make it to the other side with you. If you're flying to Chicago from Georgia, a flight on a 747 may cost you $97. There are over 400 seats on that plane. If you were flying in a jet, that jet may have 10 seats and cost over $20,000.

The same that goes with your friends. As you are moving up in your life, the same number of people won't go with you. It will hurt and sting, but you won't die. You will come to life!

Destiny is inside the decision. God knows us so well that He would hide our destiny inside of a thing we wouldn't normally face in order to make us address areas of our life that would have gone unresolved had we gotten success too soon.

Your destiny is hidden in the dungeon of your soul and in your darkest place. It's like a small seed waiting to be discovered.

When you choose to do the work and start unlayering who you thought you were, you'll have a clearer vision of where your destiny is hidden. Many people are so distracted with the small and petty problems of their lives, that they never get to the big decision.

Do you have the courage to face and resolve the darkest part of yourself and work to get the seed? Once you do that, you'll have to plant the seed and nurture it. Growing into the person you were meant to be, you'll have the ability and credibility to speak to others that have dark places identical to yours.

You will now be able to serve them and assist them with unlayering. You'll also be able to give them the courage to make the decision to enter their dark place and get their seed. Will you start today?

If you're going to go the distance, it's going to require three things: an uncomfortable yes, an uncommon commitment, and an unyielding faith.

Are you willing to go the distance with God and Become everything you were meant to be? It won't be comfortable. You will be uncomfortable for an extended period of time and possibly look like a fool. When Marconi said he could send radio signals through the air without wires in 1895, they tried to have him committed to an insane asylum.

The uncommon commitment will be relentlessness like you've never experienced before. All of your energy, time and attention will have to be about bringing the dream to pass. You can't afford to be distracted with the petty worries of life. You will lose friends, you may stop talking to some family and you'll have to work endlessly not knowing when it will come to pass.

Unyielding faith is believing in the vision no matter what your circumstances look like. It's working UNTIL the dream comes to pass. You won't know exactly how, who will show up or what will happen, you just know that it will. Why? Because God said it would.

Nobody can help a broken person like a person that was broken that God put back together again.

Amen! Amen! And Amen!!!!! Who are you getting your advice from? Someone who's as broken as you or someone who's been broken in the area you're broken and has healed? People with similar brokenness and dysfunctions tend to hang out together. Get around some whole people.

You may feel uncomfortable around them initially, as you think you have nothing to offer, but watch them show up and love you until you love yourself.

Chapter 6

Neville Goddard

I discovered Neville Goddard two years ago after listening to Earl Nightengale's 30-minute audio, *The Strangest Secret.* I've listened to this audio thousands of times and he recommended several authors. I finally decided to do some research and found an audio of Neville Goddard on YouTube. It blew my mind!!! I referred him to my family and friends around the world and they have been blown away too. I got his book and audiobook of *The Power of Unlimited Imagination,* and have listened to it countless times.

Neville Goddard is a spiritual and meta-physical teacher and if your mind is limited to religion and the way you think you may know God, you aren't ready to receive the information he shares. But if you're ready to see yourself and God in a different light, get his books and audiobooks and/or listen to his live recordings on YouTube. You will discover things about yourself that you never knew. Fascinating!

*Born on Barbados in the British West Indies in 1905, Neville Goddard came to the U.S. to study drama when he was 17. He worked in department stores in New York and later became a dancer at theaters. Under unusual circumstances, he met a black Jew, named Abdullah, who lectured on Christianity. Neville went to see him and as he waited for the lecture to begin, Addullah, whom he had never met, came down the aisle from the rear of the auditorium to the stage.

He said, "You are late, Neville! Six months late! I have been told to expect you." After that, Neville studied with Abdullah seven days a week for seven years and learned Hebrew, The Kabbalah and more about Christianity than anyone had ever taught him.

He eventually gave up theater and devoted his studies to mysticism and began his lecture career in New York. He gave a series of talks on television and lectured regularly to sold out audiences. Neville Goddard was an influential New Thought Teacher for decades. He spoke of God in intimate terms as though he knew God very well, which he did. He died in 1972.
(source NevilleGoddard.www.hubs.com and lectures)
******

If you have a secret affection for your conflicts, you cannot be helped.

Some people love to be in conflict and turmoil. They are addicted to it and won't know who they are without it. The only way to solve conflict is to acknowledge that you have a problem, make a decision to change and then take appropriate action.

Complaining about your issues every single day or telling the tragic story of your childhood to anyone that's willing to listen is not appropriate action. People are willing to spend more money on alcohol and wine, rather than attend events or read books that will assist them with their problems.

If you've been telling the same stories for the past few years and haven't taken action to change your circumstance, you need to ponder, "Do I have a secret affection for my conflicts?"

If you are honest with yourself, you will find an internal being you're not proud of. A monster that needs taming. Tame that monster by filling your mind with positive thoughts of joy and fulfillment and you will turn that monster into a being of love.

When I heard Neville Goddard say this and he died three years before I was born, I knew that I was not alone with this challenge. I was not a monster, per say, but had a tyrannical voice running loose in my head, that made me have distorted vision of myself. It was fed with negativity, drama, challenges and naysayers.

After acknowledging that I was not the voice in my head (thanks to Eckhart Tolle), I started working on it. Over time and with extensive work, the voice has been tamed. It's no longer a tyrant, but a being of love. I share this because if it could happen for me, it can happen for you too.

Stop looking at others and start observing your own reactions to their behaviors.

How easily can someone steal your joy? When you get to work, does the same person make you mad every day? How many times are you angry before 10am? If the same person makes you mad every day, how is this their problem?

When someone can control your reactions and how you respond to them, they can manipulate you. It's almost like you're a puppet and they're pulling your strings. That should make you angry...but not at them, at yourself for allowing them to do that to you. Yes, you are allowing them to manipulate you because you are giving them what they want; drama. Maybe they have a secret affection for conflict and they use their time to impose their conflicts on others.

How long will you be their likely victim? Instead of looking at others as the source of your pain, stress, and headaches, start to observe your reactions. Then, dig into your past and figure out what the root cause is to your reaction. It's rarely that person and is likely some pain point from your past you haven't resolved. Only then, will you be free to live your life.

What would you feel like if now you were the man you want to be?

What would your life look like today if you were the person that you wanted to be? How would you feel? How would others feel about you? What would you be doing?

The challenge with getting a clear vision of who you want to be is you're constantly focused on your past and how it shaped your present circumstances. You're lost in who you are and who did you wrong, and when you add that tyrant voice in your head, it's a recipe for misery.

Some people work hard their entire lives to be able to afford expensive things, only to find that they didn't make them feel the way they wanted to feel. Some people have plastic surgery to look different and then discover that they still don't feel the way they thought they would feel. So they continue to change the way they look when what they are seeking is a feeling that cannot be altered with a knife or laser.

Give yourself 30 minutes to an hour of uninterrupted time and really get clear on how you want to FEEL. Not on what you want that will get you to the feeling, but how you want to feel. God will make the way to get you to the feeling, and it won't be in the way you imagined.

How do you want to feel? Loveable, loving, loved, stress free, beautiful, inner peace, joy, free from depression, handsome, whole, healthy, drama free, financially free?

Once you get clear on how you want to FEEL, spend five to ten minutes a day living from the space of that person. This is especially helpful when you're having a bad moment. Lean back in your chair and imagine that you are this person. The more and more you practice feeling like this person, you will soon BECOME that person. It's magical.

Will you give it a go? What do you have to lose, rather than a person who you no longer desire to be?

**If you want to get clarity on where you are in life and the areas you need to work on, get my free Work-Life Balance assessment at www.christyrutherford.com/worklife

If my idea of God does not bring forth within me the sense of love, then I have the wrong God.

In the name of God and religion, there are people who protest at the funerals of fallen soldiers and gay people. They criticize unwed mothers and divorced couples. They stand outside football games and other large events protesting people who don't fit into their box of who God is and what the Bible says.

I won't resort to name calling here, but people who do stuff like this have their own view of who God is, but don't represent the whole of society. To protest someone's funeral where they are hurting and in pain from losing a family member, that's not love. That's hate in one of the highest forms.

God is love and when you are connected to God, you'll have love for yourself and others.

Life will become easier, when you are brutally frank with yourself and acknowledge your reactions to that which was created by you and is being reflected to you.

Do you create the negative situations in your life and then spend time complaining about them? The day that you take 100 percent responsibility for everything that happens to you, the good and bad, your whole life will change.

There are laws that govern the universe that are as absolute as the Law of Gravity. Two such laws include the Law of Attraction and Karma. These laws are at work every single day whether you know they exist or not.

If you watch dramatic reality shows and listen to negative music, does your life somehow mirror what you watch and listen to? Do you harshly judge and criticize others verbally or on social media and then wonder why people talk about you?

Once you realize that what you are reacting to was created by you and being reflected to you (mirror), it starts to make you more mindful about your behavior towards others. Start to monitor the negativity you inflict on others and how that shows back up in your life. The good news is that these laws also work for the good. When you serve others, and are kind to them, people will be kind and willing to serve you. Be positive and watch the impacts you make in the lives of others show up in your life. In order to cancel out and minimize the negative, do more good.

If you want to know what love is, you must become loving, for you cannot know a thing until you are it.

True love is hard to find, but only because most of us seek true love from someone else before we seek it within ourselves. If you don't truly love yourself, there is no amount of love that anyone else can give you that will be sufficient enough to satisfy you. If you are looking for someone to complete you, then you are admitting you're incomplete. If you can't seem to find love, start with loving yourself and in time, you will become loveable.

A man is sick, because he is conscious of being so. Let the sick man say, "I am well." The hungry man say, "I am full" and the troubled man say, "I am at peace," and their right consciousness will produce what they are conscious of being.

I first developed arthritis when I was 25 years old. I felt sorry for myself and cried privately at home regularly. Only a select few people knew I had it, but no one knew how much I suffered. After a year, I thought to myself, "Crying and feeling sorry for myself hasn't changed anything. I have to do something different."

I didn't know about Neville Goddard or the Law of Attraction, but I knew that I was created for greatness and wasn't meant to be crippled my entire life. The Law of Attraction works whether or not you know it exists. I started to imagine that I was healthy. I hung up pictures of fit and healthy people on my refrigerator, which was a signal that one day I would be able to run again. I stopped acknowledging I had a condition and started to study natural remedies to cure it. I also prayed to God, even though I was an atheist. I only pictured, acknowledged and talked about health.

Within six months, I put the arthritis into remission and over a 12-year period, I controlled it naturally until it showed up again in the story I referred to earlier. Only now, I knew it was stress induced and that went into my decision to leave.

This works for an illness, troubles, peace and anything you need. Everything in your life starts and ends with what follows the words I AM. Make sure you are only saying and thinking about what you want to be.

When you think of another, you are only seeing your opinion of him. If you think he is kind, he is kind. If you think he is stupid, he is stupid. As he is playing the part you have assigned him, because of your opinion of him.

What do you think about people and are you stunned that they're usually what you think of them? Is it really true or just your perspective? Choose to only see the good in people and you will be amazed by how many good people there are in the world.

To be transformed, the whole basis of your thoughts must change. But your thoughts cannot change unless you have new ideas, for you think from your ideas. All transformation begins with an intense, burning desire to be transformed. The first step in the 'renewing of the mind" is desire. You must want to be different before you can begin to change yourself. Then you must make your future dream a present fact.

Many people work but only look forward to the weekends, federal holidays and vacations. They look at their calendars and hope that time will pass quickly so that the NFL season would start and they could get their blood flowing for a few months, while rooting for their favorite team. While on vacation, they have epic fun for a few days and on the way home say, "Back to reality."

Is this really considered life? Are we dead while we're alive because we aren't working where we are meant to be and in a manner where our souls are on fire every single day?

What actions can you take that would make your life exciting and worth living every day, not just when you're off from work. What can make your work meaningful? If you are a walking zombie at work, consider changing jobs or careers. Even if you make less money because the money isn't making you happy anyway. Go NOW!!

Chapter 7

Sarah Jakes-Roberts

After Pastor Touré Roberts was hosted by TD Jakes at the Potters House last year, I started watching his videos on YouTube. He's married to Sarah Jakes-Roberts and I saw that she also had messages. After watching one of her videos, I couldn't believe how open she was about her past and brokenness. One of her earlier messages, "He Loves Me," featured her at a women's conference at a church in Maryland, and she wore a leather dress with high knee boots. I loved it because she was far from what a "featured church speaker" would dress like. I felt like she was finally comfortable with herself as a person and wasn't looking to conform to a role that she didn't want to be in.

Her willingness to open up and share the darkness of her past to assist other broken people inspired me to be vulnerable and share my insights in the books I released earlier this year. I noted that once you've been healed from your brokenness and no longer live in fear of people judging you for it, you should share that information to help other people in pain. She's an incredible person and I'm happy that she's sharing her insight with the world.

*Twenty-eight-year-old Sarah Jakes Roberts was born in West Virginia and moved to Dallas with her family. She is the daughter of Bishop TD Jakes and First Lady Serita Jakes. Despite being raised in the church and her father preaching the gospel, Sarah became pregnant at 13 years old.

A naturally gifted scholar, Sarah graduated high school early and was in the top ten percent of her class and in the nation. She attended Texas Christian University at the age of 16 and studied journalism. She dropped out of college and started waitressing at a strip club to support herself since her family had a rule that they would only support her if she was in school.

When she was 19, she married an NFL player and had another baby. They divorced four years later. She shared how he got another woman pregnant and she once confronted a woman who waited on her husband in a car outside of their house. She then got into their car and started ramming cars and was nearly arrested.

Being a teenage mom and divorced, she felt ostracized from church and didn't feel like she fit in. She started a blog to share her brokenness, withholding her last name and had three million hits in three months. Later, she met Pastor Touré Roberts, and they married in 2014.

Sarah is the senior editor of eMotions, an online inspirational magazine for women. She's also the project manager for the Rx Connection Card and was responsible for grassroots marketing efforts for the feature film, "Not Easily Broken." An author of three books, Sarah has received many honors, including recently being celebrated as a National Overcomer by Pat and Emmitt Smith Charities in partnership with *Good Morning America* co-host, Robin Roberts. She's also been featured on *The Today Show, Dr. Phil, Essence, The Associated Press*, and *The 700 Club*.

Alongside her husband, Touré Roberts, Sarah pastors a dynamic community of artists and professionals at One Church Los Angeles. They have a blended family of six children.
******

Maybe I was trying to comfort my misery and God was trying to confront it.

When you are comfortable in your misery, you aren't serving anyone. Sometimes God will make you confront your misery and resolve it. Only then will you be able to serve others. Are you willing to confront the very thing you've been running away from for years? Instead of seeking more money or a bigger house, start to seek wholeness.

Some people can become so dependent on you being their resource that they cease to be resourceful for themselves.
How much time do you spend on the phone nursing a person who has a problem in their life? Are you the person that everyone calls first when they have a problem, knowing that you will listen and perhaps offer meaningful advice? How long has this been going on and how long do you want it to continue?

If you are always there for them and soothe them in their woe-is-me stories, and they NEVER take action, why would they? Some people used to solve their problems but stopped doing so knowing they will get comfort from you.

It's time to pull your resources back in and use them to get to your destiny. You may be called selfish, but in a sense, you have to become selfish in order to fulfill the vision in your heart. No one is going to give you permission to do so. Take charge of your life and do it yourself!

Until we forgive ourselves, we will always see ourselves through the shattered pieces of the dreams we can no longer have. Nothing can be seen clearly through broken pieces: no future, no hope, no faith, no love is capable of being seen properly until we admit that we are driving on a flat tire. We have to stop believing that just because we are damaged we are irreparably broken.
Everybody who has achieved something outside of mediocrity has a story to tell. Many people don't take the time to research or listen to a person's back story. They only see their success. If this can happen for them, it can happen for you too. It starts with the moment you forgive yourself for the past, which you cannot change, and start focusing on your future.

The people with the most to offer others are those who have had the most dysfunctional pasts and healed them. If they can heal themselves, you can too. Start with forgiving yourself and then forgive those who hurt you. Your life will never be the same.

Are you willing to let go of what you want, and accept that God may have something that requires you to hurt a little?

As discussed earlier, when you're walking your path, you will be uncomfortable. When you're walking your path, you will lose some friends, family will criticize you and people will talk about you. None of these feel good and will hurt. Can you handle the pain that's associated with bringing the vision of your heart to life? As you survive each test, the pain won't be as bad as you look back. Keep moving through the pain and you'll come out on the other side to joy.

Dear God, I thought the only way you could use me was if I did everything right. Thank you for showing that my brokenness gave you more to use, not less. I spent so long trying to reject what you were trying to bless. I welcome every battle and invite every struggle. I know when it's over you'll use every scar I learn to love. Signed Learning what matters.

This is such a great expression of what grace feels like. Grace is knowing that even when you're not perfect and you're still doing things wrong, God still loves you and can use you. Grace is knowing that every battle and struggle brings a new level of joy, so it is worth overcoming. Grace is when you learn to love what once caused you so much pain. Once you experience grace, it's a feeling that you'll never want to let go of. Learning how to live in grace is what matters.

What God has for you may look like confusion to people around you. Very few people will understand what God is doing in your life, even your family.

In the early 1900's, Napoleon Hill agreed to work for Andrew Carnegie (the richest man in America) for 20 years to come up with a success philosophy. He agreed to do this for free and people thought he was nuts. Most of his family laughed at him and thought he had lost his mind, with the exception of his step-mother. His story is so amazing. His failures, triumphs, heartbreak and ultimate success over that period have changed the lives of millions of people all over the world.

His books, philosophies, and videos are still impacting people nearly 100 years after he completed them and long after he died. Napoleon Hill will continue to impact people and their families for generations to come. People won't understand what you see clearly, and that's okay. Keep moving forward.

God wastes nothing, so use what He has given you as fuel for your soul's journey.

There are no wasted moments when you're on your journey. When you understand this, you'll cherish the good times and find the lessons in the hard times. There is a seed in every "perceived" failure. I say perceived because failure is meant to teach you something. Use it all and look for the good, even in seemingly bad times. If you don't quit, you will eventually see the vision of your heart.

Why is it important for you to recognize that destiny separates you because if you aren't careful, you'll turn your destiny into a democracy and you'll be waiting for approval.

If you put your destiny up for negotiation and the support of others before you move forward, you won't take the first step. This can't be said enough, people will not support you. Knowing that nearly every leader in this book has said it in a different way, should give you comfort when you defy what others think you should do and live the life you desire. Go NOW!

Wouldn't it be lovely if we didn't have to learn before we grow... God can't do nothing with you if you know it all.

When I left my previous career, I thought I knew everything. I had a super huge ego and you couldn't tell me anything. After falling down a few times, being hustled and discovering that I had 1000's of blind spots, I surrendered to the fact that I didn't know ANYTHING. Lol!

When I let go of everything I thought I knew, I was able to open myself up to the information that I needed to know that would guide me to my destiny. Be willing to lay your ego on the altar and submit to not knowing what you don't know. It will make the journey less painful and get you to your destination quicker.

We stay with people until their contamination becomes our disease and now we're both in need of healing.
Are you in a toxic relationship? Does that person who used to take your breath away with love now take your breath away with despair? It may be time to reassess how long you will stay in a relationship that is draining your soul.

Chapter 8

Steven Furtick

I first saw Pastor Steven Furtick when he was hosted by TD Jakes at The Potter's House. Needless to say he was AMAZING and I was moved by his message. I started watching his other messages on his church's (Elevation Church) YouTube channel.

One of the things I love about Steven Furtick is his ability to relate Biblical principles into everyday life with humor and plain language. He's hilarious and down to earth. When I say plain language, I mean, you don't have to be a Bible scholar to understand his messages. They're easy to understand and implement into your everyday life.

Easy, does not mean without depth. He has a gift to teach and that is evident by the significant growth of his church. The work they do in the community and around the world is equally impressive. He has made a significant impact in the lives of people around the world and mine. He's AWESOME!

*Larry Stevens "Steven" Furtick Jr. was born in 1980 and raised in Moncks Corner, SC. He felt called to pastor a church as a teenager, and the leader of his church asked him to lead the youth's bible study when he was 16. The pastor told his parents that Steven had a gift to preach. He went to college and received a B.A. in Communications and later a Masters of Divinity.

He often talks about the strained relationship with his father. It caused a lot of pain in his family and hurt him, since he didn't understand why he was being rejected by someone who once loved him so much. They later discovered his father suffered from ALS (Lou Gehrig's Disease), which caused him to a distance himself from his wife and children.

After serving as a music director at a local church, he started Elevation Church with his wife, Holly Furtick, and seven other families in Matthews, NC. They started at a local high school. In their first service, they had 121 people.

Steven masterfully utilizes technology to leverage his time and multiplies his effectiveness in reaching people. He personifies the multi-site church concept and has 14 different locations across North Carolina, Virginia, Florida, and Toronto. He's been noted in *Outreach Magazine* as being one of the fastest growing churches in the U.S. and has nearly 20,000 people attending the 14 different locations.

Since 2006, Elevation Church has given more than $100 million to local and global outreach partners. His church members have also volunteered hundreds of thousands of hours in community service. Some of his community, national and international initiatives include packing more than 10,000 sandwiches for the homeless, helping single mothers get their cars serviced, donating blood, cleaning up parks and streets, building a soccer field for local ministries and renovating buildings, building houses, stocking food pantries, feeding the hungry and homeless, and holding a senior prom for elderly nursing home residents.

In honor of the release of one of his books, he gave away more than 2,200 book bags filled with school supplies, one bag for every book sold. The book bags were distributed throughout the U.S. and in the U.K. Hundreds more were sent to the Gulf region in the wake of Hurricane Isaac.

The contributions that Steven Furtick have made go on and on. He's published four *New York Times* bestsellers and travels all over the world sharing his insight and inspiration. He and his wife, Holly Furtick, have three children.

******

Stop wasting your potential in areas that are not related to your purpose.

How long are you going to hold on to that 9-5 while you work your dream part-time? What's more important, living in the fullness of your destiny or maintaining your luxurious lifestyle?

Keeping the lifestyle would be okay if your job wasn't choking you out.

I'm simply asking a question out of experience and I often hear many people say, "One day I'm gonna go all in." You can't dip your toe in the water if you want to get on the road to destiny and live your purpose. As some point, you're going to have to go all in. It's up to you how long you will wait for the perfect moment or until you've accumulated multiple retirements to finally do what you were meant to do. You're naïve to think that tomorrow is guaranteed.

The problem with blaming haters for what you can't do, is there is somebody else who has more haters than you and yet somehow they found a way to produce.

Ahhhh, people who blame their haters for not allowing them to move forward in their lives. This is really just about not wanting to fail and look bad in front of others. If you're afraid of what others will say or think about you if you fail, then you're not ready for your destiny. Failing is a part of the journey.

The root of your disappointment is your own dysfunction and if you can fix your own dysfunction, you can deal with any disappointment.

Steven Furtick said a mouthful here!! Once you're able to resolve what's going on within you, you won't have as many problems or issues as you do now. The root of most of your problems and disappointments are one or two large dysfunctions that you either fail to acknowledge exist or refuse to address. Solve the biggest problems in your life and the small ones will go away. Then, nothing can disappoint you.

It might surprise you what the people that you envy are actually dealing with.

Do you scowl at people who drive past you in your dream car? Do you ride by your dream house and secretly wonder how they could afford it? Do you see people who are happy and hope that they fall down the stairs?

As stated earlier, everyone is going through something. It may not be the same thing that you're going through, but they have something. Maybe they've just been laid off and are trying to figure out how they're going to make their next car payment. Maybe that happy person that you see is caring for an elderly parent and their outing is the one day they get to themselves. Maybe they're fighting cancer and have learned how to find joy in the small things.

Life is about perspective and if you shift your focus from envying others and actually address what's going on with you, your life will shift in new and exciting ways.

Conflict isn't your greatest barrier, complacency is. The only barrier you have to break is the barrier of unbelief.

Have you become comfortable with being uncomfortable and blaming others for why you aren't living the life you desire. I've heard so many people talk about how "they" won't let them live their lives, yet continue to talk to these people every single day. They've become comfortable with blaming others for not stepping out on faith and facing their greatest fears in order to fulfill their destiny.

Am I talking about you? If so, what have you learned about yourself from reading this book and what will you do differently?

Regret is what I did that's distracting me from what I'm supposed to do. Resentment is what you did that's distracting me from what I'm supposed to do.

Regret and resentment is trying to drive your life's car forward, but you keep looking in the side mirrors to see what's going on behind you or what's approaching to sabotage you.

No matter how hard you try, how long you think about it or how much you talk about it, you cannot and I mean **CANNOT change your past!** There is nothing that you can do to make it better or rearrange what could have happened.

Keep your sights focused on your future and leave your past in the past. Forgive yourself for what you didn't do and let go of regret. Then, forgive others for what they did and let go of resentment. Turn that negative energy into positive energy and use it to fuel your destiny.

Often the things that embarrass you about yourself are the very things that God has empowered you with to make a difference in your world.

Your weirdness is your greatness unrealized. The trait that made you feel like a weirdo for the majority of your life and what may have embarrassed you is your greatest gift. It is your unique identifier. Instead of looking at it in a negative light, shift your perspective and see the beauty of it. Then use it to propel yourself forward.

You can always find someone to cuddle with in your comfort zone.

This can be readily seen on social media. When someone tells a sob story, talk about their problems or their haters, there are 100's of people who are ready and willing to offer advice, prayers or support to get them through their trying times. But when someone says they started a new business or have something positive to share, they get crickets (silence). Perhaps a few likes and congratulations, but not nearly as many when they are negative.

If you want to be comfortable and don't want to step into your destiny, that's okay. Everyone is not going to answer the call and finish the race. Just realize, it was your decision, and not the fault of others.

Control is what you think you have. Control is always an illusion. The thing that life will teach you after a while is you're never really in control. It's just a matter of what it's going to take to show you that.

As a leader, being out front, we must make sure that everyone is playing their role and doing their part to move the agenda forward, so naturally we become control freaks. Leaders drive results by getting people to do what needs to be done. The problem is when we try to drive every result in our professional and personal life and don't react well when we can't. I can write an entire book on being in control and what it took to show me that I wasn't.

Being controlling can be a painful experience when you're walking towards your destiny, because it means you're still trying to drive the results you want for yourself, and not surrendering to the results that God has for you. It's humbling, painful, enlightening and a learning process.

Learning to open your hands and know that everything has a reason and a purpose in your life will allow you to believe in a plan that you don't have the full picture of. It's tough but possible.

Some of the seasons of your greatest developments will be the same as your most diabolical attacks.

When you feel like you're under pressure or attack, there is something you are meant to learn about yourself. If you feel like you are going in circles or feel like the weight of the world is going to crush you, what decision are you unwilling to make?

I knew that I was not on the right path in my career for a number of years, but wanted to retire first and have the security of a pension before I got on my path to destiny. I was sacrificing my destiny for money. Although I continued to make significant impacts in my career, I was not in the right place. I wanted to impact several hundred, God wanted me to impact several million.

The crushing and pressure made me TAKE ACTION. Looking back, it was all a part of The Plan, but at the time, I didn't know what was going on and felt betrayed, hurt and was in significant pain. As I've grown in my relationship with God and understand what it takes to walk in destiny, I forgave everyone and see the story of my despair in a different light.

If you are in pain, make a decision and take action and you too will be able to see in hindsight how that situation was meant to change you, not kill you.

Romans 5:3-5 (NIV) - Not only so, but we also glory in our sufferings, because we know that suffering produces perseverance; perseverance, character; and character, hope.

Chapter 9

Iyanla Vanzant

I watched Iyanla Vanzant periodically over the years, but a good friend hounded me for months to get her book, *Forgiveness*. I told him, "Yeah, yeah, I've been working with Oprah and others on forgiveness for years, I'm good." Finally succumbing to his requests, I got the book December 2014. THIS BOOK CHANGED MY LIFE!!!

Forgiveness is not just a book that you read, it's a book that you experience. Iyanla Vanzant uses meditation and the technique of tapping to release the negative energy from your body. I didn't realize how much toxicity and negative energy I carried around until it was gone. I didn't know how much buried resentment I had for others until I did the work to uncover it. This book is a 21-day experience and takes work. I can honestly say that I haven't had any notable headaches or general pain since releasing the negative energy from my body.

This book is a gift to the world and will save your life. Get it, do the work and free yourself from the bondage of your past. She also has videos of her appearances on YouTube. I highly recommend you watch them.

*An inspirational speaker, lawyer, New Thought spiritual teacher, author, life coach and television personality, Rev. Dr. Iyanla Vanzant was born in Brooklyn in the back of a taxi to an alcoholic mother in 1953. She was the product of an extra marital affair. After her mom died from breast cancer when she was two years old, Iyanla and her brother were left to be raised by her father, who left them in the care of a series of relatives.

She was raped by her uncle at 9 years old and by the time she was 16, she had a baby. At 21, she had 3 children and a physically abusive husband. Nine years, 2 suicide attempts and many beatings later, she left in the early morning with her 3 children to an unknown future.

She used public assistance to sustain her family for several years and ended up going to college. After graduating Summa Cum Laude from Medgar Evers College in Brooklyn, she went to the City University of New York Law School at Queens College. After a brief career as a lawyer, she realized she made the wrong career choice and left the practice.

She eventually started appearing on Oprah and wrote several best-selling books. She also had her own talk show. However, in 2002, her talk-show was canceled, she lost millions of dollars, her husband left and her daughter died of cancer the following year. She suffered from devastating depression and contemplated suicide. After reuniting with Oprah in 2011, she got her own show, "Iyanla, Fix My Life," which is the #1 reality show on OWN.

Over the past 30 years, Iyanla has published 15 books, including 6 *New York Times* bestsellers, selling over 8 million copies translated into 23 languages. She's received an Emmy and numerous accolades and awards from magazines, including "One of the Country's Most Influential African Americans" from *Ebony* Magazine in 2004 and "One of the Country's Most 100 Influential Women" from *Women's Day* Magazine 2003.

(source Iyanla.com and IMDB)

******

If you don't love what you're doing, run for your life.

Be selective about your job and don't just take one for security. There is nothing worse than feeling like you are wasting away at a job you hate.

Sometimes you may have to work a job you dislike to get to your dream job, but make sure you are constantly moving towards your goals. Don't stay stagnate in a job that you don't desire and then complain about it every day over alcoholic drinks.

What would you do every day if all of your lifestyle expenses were paid? What problem do you want to solve for the world? Seek a job or mission within those areas and it will bring you immense joy and freedom.

Whatever you attach I AM to, you will become.

As we've moved through this book, you should be aware of the power of your words. What do you say about yourself regularly? "I am broke." "I am crazy." "I am fat." I am sick."

Everything that you say about yourself, you become. Start to become more mindful about the words you're speaking over your life and what's showing up in your life. When you see the negative scenarios you've created with your words, you know that the theory is true. Now use it for the positive. "I am healthy." "I am financially secure." "I am loved." "I am at my perfect weight." Watch your words and observe how your life will shift in a positive way.

Never judge your clarity based on how other people respond.

How often are you frustrated that people don't see your vision as clearly as you? Are you frustrated when you describe your dreams to others and they don't see how easy it is for you to do? Spending time trying to convince people of what you see is a waste of time. It's been said time and time again throughout this book, and mainly because it's a huge hurdle that you need to overcome.

No one is going to give you permission to be happy. You have to own that for yourself! When your vision is clear, it's because you are adequately prepared from everything that you've been through in your life. All of your experiences, the good and bad, have prepared you for what you are meant to do. Sharing your vision with others and expecting for them to see it clearly is unrealistic, because although they may know you, they have not walked a mile in your shoes.

They aren't looking through the same lenses that your lifetime of experience has provided. Move forward without the support and ignore the naysayers. Bring your vision to full fruition and once they see it, they will understand.

Be authentic. Many people don't know what that means. Be authentic means you're in integrity. That what you think, what you say, what you feel and what you do all matter.

Not being authentic is when you've forgotten who you are in an effort to become who everyone else wants you to be. Bending and conforming to meet the needs of other people. Remaining authentic is increasingly difficult for leaders because of the number of hats leaders wear.

Leadership is not only expected on the job, you are a leader everywhere you go, and because of that, you become 10 different people. One person in front of your peers, another in front of our employees, another in front of your bosses, one in front of your family, another in front of your kids, another as a youth coach.

Authenticity is being one person serving 10 roles. Can you afford to act any other way than you're expected to act in your role at work? Have you lost the qualities that made you unique and happy?

Have you sold your soul and given away pieces of who you are for success and wonder why you're not happy? Would your high school classmates and coworkers tell the same stories about you? Authenticity is your 7th grade self. Before high school and peer pressure. Before you were swayed by the opinions of others and before life put a whooping on you.

True authenticity is existing from a space where you can be yourself and not apologize for who you are. Don't apologize for being awesome. Stand in who you are and know exactly who you are. Don't change to make other people feel comfortable. You are good enough just as you are and if people don't like it, they are welcomed to leave your life.

Your willingness to look at your darkness is what empowers you to change

Are you willing to look inside of yourself at the thing you have been running away from for an extended period of time and resolve it? Are you willing to admit your greatest dysfunction and work to resolve it? We all have a chapter in our life's book that we don't share with anyone. However, when we are in relationships, marriages, under stress or any other time we're pressured, it oozes out and sparks a fire.

What resentment are you holding on to from your childhood? What happened to you in your past that you haven't forgiven yourself or others about? When you have the courage to make the choice to look into that dark space, you'll find that your seed of destiny is right there waiting for you. When you resolve the darkest part of your life, you now have the ability to use your story to help others resolve theirs. That's the greatest gift you can give yourself and the world.

Comparison is an act of violence against the self.

Social media has allowed people to see into the lives of others and you may be making unfair comparisons of your life with the people you are connected to. Do you compare your house and car to your friends, and then wonder how they can afford what they have, while beating yourself up for not being able to afford it? Do you look at the lifestyle of celebrities and wish you were them, because of the material possessions they have? Do you look at the marriage of others and wish you were like couples who smile in all their pictures?

How do you know that what you are seeing from others is true? You are looking at what they show you, but have no idea of what their reality is. Just like no one else knows what's really going on in your house. Every minute that you spend looking at someone and what they have, it leaves you one less minute to be grateful for what you have. Redirect your attention from others and look at how you can become greater. That's where true happiness begins.

You can accept or reject the way you are treated by other people, but until you heal the wounds of your past, you will continue to bleed. You can bandage the bleeding with food, with alcohol, with drugs, with work, with cigarettes, with sex, but eventually, it will all ooze through and stain your life. You must find the strength to open the wounds, stick your hands inside, pull out the core of the pain that is holding you in your past, the memories, and make peace with them.

As referenced in the earlier pages, Iyanla's book, *Forgiveness* will change your life. When you're able to work to forgive yourself and others, it will free you from so much inner turmoil and pain, that your life will never be the same.

So many people self-medicate their issues and don't know they can change. I'm here to tell you that there is a remedy to what you are seeking. Get her book and give yourself the gift of FREEDOM! It will liberate you!

When you need to be loved, you take love wherever you can find it. When you are desperate to be loved, feel love, know love, you seek out what you think love should look like. When you find love, or what you think love is, you will lie, kill, and steal to keep it. But learning about real love comes from within. It cannot be given. It cannot be taken away. It grows from your ability to re-create within yourself, the essence of loving experiences you have had in your life.

Learning to love yourself is a gift. When you learn to love yourself, you will love everything and everyone around you. People won't annoy you as much, the air will be fresher, skies bluer and food will taste better. People will flock to you and desire to have what you have, not realizing you just love yourself. They will want that too.

You have to set standards for how you want to be treated and what you expect from yourself and for yourself.

As you've moved through this book, you may have realized that there are some people you are going to have to leave behind.

When you start to love yourself, you will realize how much crap you've put up with from other people. When you don't fully love yourself, having crap friendships and relationships are normal.

As you move towards self-acceptance and self-love, the same behavior that you put up with for years will no longer be tolerable to you. "They" will say that you've changed and for the most part, you have. You will be responsible for training people on how you want to be treated and not accepting anything less than the best.

So many of us invest a fortune making ourselves look good to the world, yet inside we are falling apart. It's time to invest on the inside.
It's time to make yourself a priority! Are you aware of what would make everyone around you happy, but don't have a clue about yourself? Do you spend your time making sure everyone else is healthy and provided good food to eat, but don't spend the same time or effort ensuring you take care of yourself? Are you the peace maker, always bringing calm to tense situations, yet get battered by the negative voice in your head?

It's time to give yourself permission to take better care of yourself, so you can better serve others. Take some time and really think about what you want your life to look like. Visualize yourself happier, with more joy and less stress and then consider what it will take to get there. What's blocking you from getting to that life? What decisions do you need to make to achieve the life you desire?

Make the choice to spend time on yourself, so you can figure out exactly what you want your life to look like and how you want to feel. If not, you'll get stuck in a perpetual cycle, and spend your time constantly fending off the things you don't desire. Stress, anxiety, and depression should not be a natural part of your life. Get clear and start at once to move in the direction of your dreams! You are worth it!

Chapter 10

Keion Henderson

I started watching Pastor Keion Henderson when he was hosted by TD Jakes at the Potter's House. I saw him last year, but after watching him a few months ago I had to study with him more. One of the things that resonated with me was the story of his childhood and all the struggles and pain he went through before becoming highly successful.

His messages are strong and like a kick in the head if you need to be shifted out of your comfort zone. He has a no-nonsense approach to teaching and doesn't hold back. I look forward to continually watching his messages and growing from them.

*Keion Henderson was born in 1981 and grew up in Gary, Indiana. Raised by a single mom who worked at Taco Bell, he and his three sisters shared a bedroom in their small apartment. He said that his younger sister had to wear his hand-me-down clothes, because his mom couldn't afford to buy a new set for her. He also shared that they didn't have money for groceries and would eat whatever leftover food his mom brought from work.

For years, his mom didn't reveal who his real father was and this created anguish for a large part of his childhood, as he cried himself to sleep at night. At night, his mom would pray over him and when he was a teenager, she started praying for him to meet TD Jakes.

One day, his mom revealed that his father was the pastor at the church they attended, which made him angry as the pastor always knew who he was, but didn't create a relationship with him.

He was called to minister when he was 14 years old. He attended college, and distinguished himself as an athlete and campus leader. He pursued a career in education, earning a designation as "One of the Top 50 Educators," in Fort Wayne, IN.

At a chance meeting in a restaurant over six years ago, he met TD Jakes. At the time, he was living in a one-bedroom apartment with his wife, as their daughters slept on the couch because they couldn't afford a larger place. After watching a few of his videos, TD Jakes told him that he was an Olympic swimmer in shallow water. He told him that he would make the right connections for him, and since then, The Lighthouse Church, in Houston, has grown over 3500 percent, to nearly 4,000 members.

His community projects include raising money for the Red Cross after the Boston bombing and West Texas chemical explosion and donating 22,500 pounds of clothes to South America and South Africa. He also owns businesses with 10 locations across the nation. Keion Henderson and his wife, First Lady Felicia Henderson, have three daughters.
******

We are born looking like our parents, but die looking like our decisions.

The decisions that you made up to this point, good and bad, have gotten you to where you are today. Many people want to blame others for their circumstances, but fail to look at how they contributed to the problem with the decisions that they made. Even if you don't make a decision, not making a decision is a decision.

When people complain about how they aren't able to get ahead in life, I ask them why didn't they go to college or if they went to college, why haven't they pursued specialized certifications. When they give the reasons on why they didn't choose to take the right action, there are other people who were in even worse situations than them that chose to defy the odds and do what needed to be done.

What decisions do you need to make in life to change your life for the best?

You don't need what you don't have.

You have everything that you need to carry out God's purpose in your life. It is all within you. As stated earlier, your greatest gifts are what you downplayed or buried to fit in with others. You don't need more money, time, resources, or people. You have what you need to start and as you take the first step, the other things will show up. It takes commitment, focus, and persistence. Those things will get you further than a million dollars.

You haven't been called until you're criticized. If nobody criticizes you, you ain't doing nothing.

I hope that this has somehow been etched in your brain, as it's a constant theme with all the leaders in this book. If no one is talking about you, that means that you aren't doing anything spectacular. If they are talking about you, hating on you and hoping that you fail, then understand that you are on the right path and are in good company. You aren't alone with this challenge.

A lot of us do things for compliments. We do things so that people can say you look good. We buy cars we cannot afford so people can say, "I like that car." What bank can you take a compliment to?

This quote pretty much says it all. Are you working, dressing, driving and living for compliments? Do you want to be the envy of your friends and the talk of the town? Do you take selfies or post pictures, only to check and see how many people responded?

I'm not sure how this became the standard or the norm in which many people live, but it's not healthy and it's not long lasting. When you live to please everyone, you're living to please no one. If you aren't pleased with yourself and who you are, no amount of compliments can fill that void. Self-love is the key.

Any worthwhile goal will look stupid before it's understood. It takes courage to stand and believe when no one else seems to understand.

To be a dreamer and a visionary is a lonely road. It takes courage to live the life that you want to live, regardless of public opinion and perception. Dr. Martin Luther King was not widely celebrated while he was alive. As the fruits of his labor started to take form and impact others after his assassination, he became more notable and celebrated.

What dream are you holding on to and refusing to unleash for the fear of looking stupid? It's time to set it free and get on your road to destiny!

That's the problem with some of you, you have big dreams and small friends. When you have big dreams and small friends, you will always acquiesce the dream to the size of your circle.

The manifestation of your dreams can never outgrow the size of your circle. It's time to get around other dreamers and visionaries. People who will speak life into your dreams and not fear. What are you waiting for?

Don't ever be so weak minded, that you allow people to make you mad at someone you don't have a problem with.

There are plenty of gossipers in the world, but do you allow people to affect your perspective of others? Remember what Neville Goddard said about a person showing up based on your opinion of them? Well, the same is true for your friends. Are your friends sharing their perspective of someone and you take their word for it and dislike the person too?

Based on what you know now, this is unwise. Give that person the benefit of the doubt and judge them for yourself with an open heart.

The level of your anointing is gauged by how you handle those who mishandle you, and if you can't handle people who mishandle you, you'll never be King.

How do you handle the people who criticize you? Do you get mad and lash back out at them? If someone cuts you off in traffic, do you get mad and give them the middle finger?

Walking with God and living in relationship is about living from a place of clarity and love. Being able to manage yourself in challenging, negative and stressful situations is what Joel Osteen talked about earlier in passing the small tests. They are tests of your character.

This is not an overnight process, and will take time to grow the discipline. It's worthy of aspiring to. Recognize that if you say you want to be more patient, God will start testing that assumption by putting people in your path that will make you angry. They will be like sandpaper and wear down your nerves until you realize that it's what you asked for.

At that moment, you will need to choose a different reaction to them and once you discipline yourself around that, and pass the small tests, you will have more patience. It's not a state that will appear in a cloud of magic dust. You have to work for it!

The problem is you're listening to people who haven't been where you're trying to go.

I've talked to so many people who are angry and resentful about the advice they are getting from others as they desire to step out of their comfort zone and play big in life. They complain, are resentful and are downright frustrated at the level of resistance they get. This usually comes from their family and friends.

When you buy someone's opinion, you buy their lifestyle, so if you wouldn't trade places with them, why are you listening to them? Can a person who's been divorced twice tell you how to have a happy marriage? Can a person who's been working at the same job for 20 years give you advice on entrepreneurship? Can someone who's never owned a home, tell you the pros and cons of owning one? Can a dentist tell you about the complications with gallbladder surgery?

Be careful about who you share your dreams and goals with. Be mindful about who you get your advice from. If they don't have the results you desire, then they aren't the right person to get advice from.

Growth is the best way to deal with dysfunction.

BECOMING a better person starts with growth. Reinvest your time from activities that are not producing the results you desire and start to do things that will make you better. Read books that address the challenges you have. Turn the television off and start watching videos of successful people.

Turn your car into a personal development university. Listen to audiobooks during your commute that have solutions to your challenges. Instead of talking on the phone and having fruitless conversations, start to look within yourself and figure out what you need to change. Go to events, seminars, and webinars and put yourself in the presence of people that have the results you desire. Your life will never be the same for the best.

Closing

I hope that this book was useful to you and valuable for the time you invested in reading it. I have learned so much from these leaders and wanted to share their insight and knowledge with more people around the world.

Most of them have books, videos, audios and a host of other resources that will assist you with the challenges that life brings. I'm so happy that you've joined me on this journey of unfolding and discovery. I 'm excited about what your future holds.

These are the links to the additional free resources I offered:
1. Free E-course – Take Inventory, get flaky people out of your life! www.christyrutherford.com/takeinventory
2. Work-Life Balance Assessment
www.christyrutherford.com/worklife
3. Free Quote cutouts – www.christyrutherford.com/quotes

Keep me informed of your progress! Send me an e-mail and connect with me on social media.
My links are:
Web: www.christyrutherford.com
LinkedIn: www.linkedin.com/in/christyrutherford
Facebook: http://www.facebook.com/christyrppc
Twitter: https://twitter.com/liveupleaders
YouTube: http://bit.ly/ChristyRYoutube
Email: liveupleadership@gmail.com

To your success, happiness and unlimited joy!!

About The Author

Christy Rutherford is a Leadership and Success Coach and President of LIVE-UP Leadership, a leadership development and training company. Christy is also a certified Executive Leadership Coach and assists companies with creating cultures of high performance.

Christy Rutherford served over 16 years as an active duty Coast Guard officer and is the 13th African American woman to achieve the rank of O-5 in the Coast Guard's 245+ year history. Her tours expanded from: drug interdictions on the high seas; emergency response/dispatch to hundreds of major/minor maritime accidents; enforcing federal laws on 100's of oil/hazardous material companies; responding to the needs of the citizens in New Orleans two days after Hurricane Katrina; a Congressional Fellowship with the House of Representatives and lastly a position that benefited from her wide range of experience.

A Harvard Business School attendee in the Program for Leadership Development, Christy also earned a Bachelor of Science in Agricultural Business from South Carolina State University, a Master of Business Administration from Averett University, a Diploma Sous Chef de Patisserie from Alain and Marie Lenotre Culinary Institute, and a Certification in Executive Leadership Coaching from Georgetown University.

Among her many professional accomplishments, her national recognition includes the Coast Guard Dorothy Stratton Leadership Award, Cambridge Who's Who Amongst Executives and Professionals, Career Communications STEM Technology All-Star and the Edward R. Williams Award for Excellence In Diversity.

A speaker and best-selling author, Christy recently released four books, *Shackled To Success, Heal Your Brokenness, Philosophies of Iconic Leaders and Philosophies of Spiritual Leaders.*

Notes

Notes

Made in the USA
Columbia, SC
19 July 2022

63698273R00057